A BROKEN PROMISE

MAXINE SUE FELLER

ISBN (Hardback):   979-8-89381-017-2
ISBN (Paperback):   979-8-89381-018-9
ISBN (eBook):   979-8-89381-019-6

508 West 26th Street KEARNEY, NE 68848
402-819-3224
info@medialiteraryexcellence.com

Contents

Chapter 1
Chapter 2
Chapter 3
Chapter 4
Chapter 5
Chapter 6
Chapter 7
Chapter 8
Chapter 9
Chapter 10
Chapter 11
Chapter 12
Chapter 13
Chapter 14
Chapter 15
Chapter 16
Chapter 17
Chapter 18
Chapter 19
Chapter 20
Chapter 21
Chapter 22
Chapter 23
Chapter 24
Chapter 25
Chapter 26
Chapter 27
Chapter 28

Chapter 1

An ominous rumble sounded in the sky. The thick dark clouds above started to release torrents of rain, but Grace Goodrich continued to vent her anger by furiously clipping at the hedges around her Victorian home while she sobbed.

Her long-time next-door neighbor, Cynthia Gilbert pulled a batch of chocolate-chip cookies from the oven, and saw grace through her kitchen window. She laid the hot pans on the counter to cool. It crossed her mind that she might be of some help to her young friend. Grabbing a large towel, and an umbrella, she hurried out the kitchen door to talk to Grace at the hedge.

"What's the matter Grace? why are you so upset?" Take this towel and come into my kitchen for a cup of tea."

Grace followed Cynthia into her kitchen. At the door Grace smelled the cookies Cynthia had baked this morning. She took a seat in the cozy kitchen at the yellow and white- checkered kitchen table.

Cynthia poured the tea. Then, she put a plate of cookies on the table and sat beside Grace while she dried her hair.

"Cynthia, I can't understand what's happening in my home anymore. My husband arranged for the honeymoon we couldn't afford when we married to take me to Paris. He told the travel agent when he wanted us to leave. It was to be two months after he retired.

Well, the travel agent called this morning to confirm it. But after they spoke George said that he'd arranged our trip…. but it's not to Paris! He isn't going to take me to Paris!"

"Is he taking someone else?"

"After they spoke, I was shocked to hear George say "Be ready to pack our clothes. I'll be driving us over to see the "Hot-air ballon Festival" Saturday in Albuquerque, New Mexico. The agent is mailing me the tickets. At my age I can't be too far from my doctor.""

"What about Paris?" … I asked him.

George replied, "I want to see the Hot-air ballon Festival in Albuquerque. At my age I don't want to be too far from my doctor."

Grace's lower lip trembled, and she blubbered, "George has never broken a promise to me before…. he knew how much I wanted to see Paris."

Then, Cynthia handed Grace another towel, and said, "Grace, i understand that you're very disappointed that George broke his promise to you.

"Cynthia, I was stunned. You know I get tongue-tied and can't speak when I'm upset. I always try to avoid scenes, and angry words. What can I say to my husband about his sudden change of mind?"

"Grace dear, last week you told me George was going to see his doctor. Did he learn something about his health that he hasn't yet told you about? It might explain why he's been repeating himself lately."

"Cynthia, you're right. George has been acting oddly lately. Three weeks ago, he left our bedroom to move into out daughter's vacated bedroom."

"Is that the reason why you've been looking so unhappy?"

"Cynthia, I thought George was cheating on me with a younger woman. I was angry, hurt, and ready to divorce him... I hired a detective to follow him and find out."

"Good grief Grace, I'm so sorry to hear that... what did he find out?"

"The detective reported to me there was no "other woman" in my husband's life. I was very glad to hear it, and the news really surprised me. Then, she sniffled, I began to wonder if it was because of my wrinkled aging body that was disgusting to George. It is to me."

"Grace, you're a beautiful woman. You should be proud of how good you look…what a heavy unnecessary burden you've been carrying around... why is it that you always assume things negatively? Grace, screw up your courage my girl. Get the facts! go to him and ask George why he moved into Linda's bedroom instead of punishing yourself with these awful untrue thoughts."

"Cynthia, men look more distinguished as they age, but women just look older. I'm fear to lose what's left of my self-respect. I fear George will agree with everything that I've been thinking."

"Well, your handsome husband doesn't look like seventy-two; the mandatory age to be retired from his company. And he does look distinguished. But Grace, you look wonderful at your age too."

"Do you really think so? Cynthia, my ego doesn't allow me to ask George why he chose to leave our bedroom. In that way I can hold onto the idea that George is punishing me for not being able to keep our daughter from running off three weeks ago with Dallas... that lanky unemployed cowboy George thought to be unworthy of his Linda, "the apple of his eye.""

Cynthia understood Grace was terribly upset, and she wondered if she'd even heard what she'd asked her? So, Cynthia asked Grace again, "Grace, you told me George was going to see his doctor. Did he learn something about his health that he hasn't told you yet? It might clear up why he's been acting... lost? and he constantly needs to repeat himself."

"Oh, dear me... do you think George has a brain tumor, or something like that?"

Grace dear, please do try to stop jumping to dire assumptions. you don't know the answers to before you ask the necessary questions, and get the facts! Please try not to jump to your conclusions without the facts in order to avoid a confrontation.

I'll watch over your house while you're gone. enjoy your trip to Albuquerque. I do hope nothing is radically wrong with George when he does reveals the results of his medical condition."

"Cynthia, thank you for helping me to realize there may be a larger problem here than George breaking a travel promise to me. This morning, I saw he confused my tube of eye –cream for his tube of toothpaste again. oh... I see it has stopped raining. I must get out of these wet clothes. Bye."

***

Grace left her friend's house and stopped at the tool shed. She wiped and hung the sheers, then hurried to her house.

Chapter 2

Grace went upstairs to her bedroom to shower and shed her wet clothes. After that, she sat at her blue- mirrored French styled vanity. As she blew her hair dry, she recalled how flattered she'd felt when George asked her to talk some sense into their daughter.

However, Linda was just as stubborn as her father, and she was not able to convince her daughter to wait until she graduated high school before she left home with Dallas…Grace wiped a tear from her eye. She missed Linda, and her son, Barry.

Those two were always devoted to one another; yet as different as night and day. Barry was a frail studious fellow who was never in trouble. While Linda was excellent in athletics, beautiful, but not smart, and always in trouble.

She was nothing like me as a young girl. I'd always obeyed whatever my mother taught me…" Don't ask questions and do as you're told!"

Suddenly, as she brushed her hair… Grace wondered why George hadn't talked to Linda himself? Why had he asked her to do it? George was a star salesman at the company where he worked. While she always did as she was told to do by her parents, and then by George. Humph. He should've been the one to speak to Linda… Yet he asked me to do it Grace said to her reflection in the mirror. George knew I would fail…better me than him?

After that, Grace opened her make-up drawer and started to fix up her face. When she was satisfied with her appearance, she reached into another drawer in the vanity for the diary her busy successful lawyer son had sent her after she'd complained to him, that she missed talking with him. It seemed to her that she was with Barry whenever she used it. It often helped her to sort out her thoughts. Dear Diary,

I'll go with George to see the hot-air ballons, but on the condition that we go to Paris, France on our next trip. I miss cuddling with George… at least we'll be back in the same bedroom. I won't bring up the subject of Linda leaving home, or Paris right now.

What's done is done… Mama used to say… "don't stir up the sh-t after it settles".

Months ago, George was so excited about arranging our trip to Paris… what could he have learned from his doctor that he hasn't told me?

***

The following morning Grace wrote:

Dear Diary,

It was amusing the first time George brushed his teeth with my eye-creme, but he continues to do it. Also, he's repeating himself even more often… George works out each day and he looks very fit… It must be hard for him to be forced to retire from his good job. He really enjoys doing it, but that's his company's policy.

Why is it men look more distinguished as they age, but women just look older?

Chapter 3

Dear Diary,

I parked in the driveway today and beeped the horn as usual to signal George to come out and help me carry in the packages. However, he didn't come out. I thought he might've fallen asleep again, and so I leaned on the horn longer… Still no George. Then, I wondered if he might be ill?

Grabbing the package filled with frozen foods I hurried inside. There was George watching a baseball game seated at the kitchen table… of course, I was relieved, but nevertheless i complained to him. "George, I need your help getting in the rest of the groceries from the car."

Immediately, he turned off the television while telling me, "The millionaire on second- base threw the ball to the millionaire on first-base, but he missed catching it. so, the multi-millionaire on the other team made the winning home run." Can George be losing his hearing?

***

Dear Diary,

George handed me the sealed envelope that arrived in the mail from the travel agency containing the "hot-air balloon festival" tickets for the opening show on Saturday. He told me that he'll be driving south to route 66 from Chicago, and then go west to Albuquerque, New Mexico. I've already packed my sexiest nightgowns.

***

The scenic drive was interesting to Grace until they reached route 66. After that there were miles and miles of long stretches of the same dying grass and low mountains on both sides of the road.

Grace tried several times to engage George in conversation, but he insisted he needed to concentrate on driving the car. She looked out the car window and pondered on the fact that she was now with her beloved husband twenty-four hours a day, yet she'd never felt this lonely in all the forty years they'd been married.

It seemed like a lot longer than three months ago since his retirement luncheon. George no longer patted or pinched her behind. His disposition had deteriorated from sweet and cheerful to downright grumpy. Nowadays they barely spoke.

Grace withdrew a cigarette from her purse and lit it while staring at the stubble on her husband's face with disgust. She'd started to smoke because she knew he didn't want her to smoke. He'd told her he was going to grow a beard. Grace wondered if it was it his way of celebrating his retirement? I will miss seeing my handsome clean-shaven husband she thought.

***

George sneaked another look at the shapely blonde beside him. He didn't recall why this woman was with him, but he was glad to have her company. He asked, "Can you find us some music on the radio?"

The woman leaned forward to turn on the radio, and search for a satisfactory station. George enjoyed peaking down her blouse as she did it. Then he said, "Must you always he switching stations?"

Grace leaned forward again to turn off the radio while thinking there's just no pleasing this man anymore. She crushed out her cigarette in the tray and opened the window, but George asked her to close it.

Even though the air conditioner was on Grace was warm, but she closed it. George doesn't care if I need to fan myself to feel more comfortable, she thought with a sigh. What's George keeping from me about his health report?

It must be responsible for his drastic change in attitude. He doesn't even say my name anymore. It makes me feel like he doesn't want to remember that he has a wife.

***

George steered the car to a vacant pump in a gas station on the side of the road. While he was pumping gas, Grace searched to find a pleasing music station.

At his farewell luncheon her husband was given a GPS, but George became upset with it as soon as he realized he'd have to listen to a female voice giving him travel directions. Grace opened her purse and pulled out another cigarette, and her diary.

Dear Diary,

George doesn't like to use his GPS. He named it "gypsy." He bickers with it whenever he uses it, and will disengage it if it says, "recalculating" more than twice. At first, I thought his behavior with gypsy was hilarious until he angrily accused me of laughing at his ineptness. Friends warned me it might take George a while to adjust to retirement, but I thought they were just teasing me.

I refused to believe he'd suffer from the "retirement blues". Could it be that? Is it something else? When will George share his medical news with me?

I've looked forward to my husband's retirement for over forty years. a time when I wouldn't be playing second fiddle to his job. However, I never anticipated we'd be getting on one another's nerves.

I'm hoping he'll get the hang of not working very soon. I miss having a pleasant companion. It's no fun to be with this grumpy old man my dear husband has become.

***

George returned to the car. "The cashier inside told me there's a nice place to eat three miles up the side-road on the right to eat. I'm hungry. I don't want the car to over-heat."

Well, Grace thought, I'm glad to hear that he's being considerate of something beside himself.

Chapter 4

George parked at the curb in front of a red building with a neon sign that said, "Cellarbration". They left the car, and George led the way. He walked from the street level down a short flight of steps to enter a basement restaurant. Grace followed him wondering if the sign had been mis-spelled, or was it a clever play on words?

He opened the door, and Grace saw the place was lit with many round white, red, green, and yellow colored paper lanterns suspended from the ceiling. Large colorful fiesta advertisements decorated the unpainted brick walls.

Suddenly, they heard the voice of Frank Sinatra blaring out from a tall antique Wurlitzer jukebox at the side of the room.

"What a beauty" George exclaimed, and they hurried over to feed it dollars and quarters. Grace searched its guide and made many selections. It occurred to her this was the first thing they'd agreed upon in many days.

He said, "It's fun picking out songs. I like to dance."

"Ah, George remembers our early romantic times together. I hope this music will stir his desire to become romantic again, and behave as he once did.

Grace noticed a tall slender man behind the bar wearing an apron but had a graduation cap on with the tassel on its left side. He was wiping the beer glasses with great care. then, she was surprised to see a short rotund man dressed in a major general uniform with the sleeves cut short approach them. His waxed mustache was curled up at the ends. he motioned them to follow him to an empty table and gave them menus after they were seated.

George whispered, "This is an unusual place. I never saw brick and stucco used for an inside wall treatment. I hope the food in here is good."

Grace liked the unusual ambiance of this restaurant, and the whimsically dressed staff. She thought it clever of the person who decorated this place to use the cheerful gay colors of a Mexican Fiesta to liven up an otherwise dark and dreary cellar. There were various shaped framed mirrors hanging on the walls which added more light and echoed the pretty colors.

***

A long- legged waitress wearing a wedding headdress, and a short French upstairs maid costume flounced over to the table to take their order. Grace noticed she'd stuffed a pillow under her blouse making it appear that she was pregnant.

George ordered, "Please bring us two rare burgers, two drafts of beer, and a side of onion rings".

As the woman walked away to place their orders in the kitchen Grace leaned forward to whisper, "Why do you think she makes herself look pregnant?"

"I don't know." George said while ogling the hemline of her short costume bouncing up and down flirtatiously as she walked toward the kitchen.

In this unusual place Grace recalled "Alice in Wonderland" when Alice tumbled down the rabbit hole and viewed all those whimsical characters; Grace was happy to see George was smiling in this place.

Grace was aware her husband didn't want to retire, and she realized he would need more time to let go his resentment at being "put out to pasture" too soon.

In this fanciful place George was starting to return to his old enthused-pleasant-self; the man Grace had agreed to marry.

A phone started ringing, and Grace looked around the room. A very pretty blonde woman seated at a table near the wall-phone answered it. After talking a few moments, she hung it up, grabbed an oversized- briefcase lying on the table in front of her, and hurried to the door.

The bartender stopped wiping the glasses and called out, "Good luck, Cindy."

The blonde turned back to him, "Thanks Jack" she said and departed.

"George, that woman was carrying the largest briefcase I ever saw."

"She's pretty enough to be a model. it's probably her resume."

As they waited for their food to be brought, they heard voices singing "Happy Birthday" beyond the pillar at the far end of the restaurant. It completely blocked a small hidden banquet area.

After the singing stopped, they heard applause and laughter. Then, a man dressed in a red devil's costume wheeled a large chocolate cake with smoke still rising from its many candles into view. He hurried to the kitchen door.

At the swinging kitchen doors, he nearly collided with a brown-haired slender woman wearing combat boots. She carried a tin tray and headed straight to their table to deliver the steaming burgers and rings.

George asked the woman for ketchup. and Grace saw the look of disappointment replace the smile on the woman's face. She lifted her burger... hesitated, and then bit into it. "This burger is the most delicious I ever tasted" Grace declared.

The cook-waitress grinned at her after that, and she went back to the kitchen. Then, the waitress brought them foaming beer in large, handled glasses.

"Aren't you glad that I took control of driving from gypsy? Otherwise, I wouldn't have found this great eating place."

On realizing her husband was in a good mood, Grace asked, "Is there something you haven't told me yet about your health George?"

"I'm fit as a fiddle. How about a dance? I miss dancing cheek to cheek."

"I've missed dancing with you, too."

They rose from the table and started to dance on the red tiled floor. However, when he pulled her close, Grace felt his scratchy beard on her face, and she pushed him away back to arm's length.

"What's the matter? don't you like dancing close to me?"

"I love dancing close with you George, but your beard feels scratchy on my face. I don't like that you grew it without asking me what I thought about your idea."

"Well, you don't ask me about the clothes you choose to wear." Tears sprang to her eyes, and Grace fled to the restroom. She didn't want to give George the satisfaction of seeing he'd hurt her feelings.

George was angry and stomped back to the table. he ordered a whiskey sour from the waitress. When it arrived, he gulped it down. Then he asked, "What do you think of my beard?"

Mindful that her tip depended on the right answer she said, "Only a virile man like you could grow such a thick beard."

Pleased with her answer, he chuckled and said, "I'll have another whiskey sour."

On returning Grace saw the emptied glasses on the table. She thought it would be futile to tell her husband he was in no condition to continue to drive. Instead, Grace lied, "George, I don't feel well. Do you mind if we stay in town overnight?"

He'd been prepared to defend his right to grow a beard but became most solicitous when he heard his companion say that she didn't feel well.

He hurried over to the bartender to ask him if he knew a place where he could rent a room for the night? The barkeep handed him a motel card.

After that, George went to the payphone. The man George spoke to didn't say a room was available when he asked, but when George mentioned he'd been given the motel's card by the

barkeep at "Cellarbration" the clerk said, "Oh, you want to come over here to continue to celebrate… right?"

George asked again, "Do you have a room?"

"Sure. Come right over."

Chapter 5

When they arrived at the motel, Grace went inside and signed the register while George parked the car, and then came to the desk. The night clerk led them to a clean room. Once inside, the clerk demonstrated how the bed could be made to vibrate. Then, he handed Grace the key, and left.

Grace gave the key to George and asked him to go back to the car and bring in their suitcases.

When George returned, he told his companion the clerk was surprised to see he'd brought in suitcases. After that, Grace started to laugh until tears rolled down her face. On seeing her laugh, George laughed too, but he had no idea why they were laughing.

***

After a restless night's sleep George awoke with a headache. He glanced at the pretty woman still asleep in their queen-size bed and saw one of her breasts had slipped out from her nightgown. George felt an urge to make love to this shapely woman and reached out to fondle her breast.

However, he recalled she'd rebuffed him because of his scratchy beard. so, he went into the bathroom to shave it off. Returning to the bed he cradled the woman in his arms and covered her with his warm moist kisses until she awoke.

On seeing his clean- shaven face Grace said, "Darling, there're quarters in my purse if you want to make the bed vibrate." After a thoroughly successful romantic encounter they showered together, and then they got dressed.

In the lobby Grace asked the day-desk clerk to recommend a place to eat.

He suggested they walk to the French style bakery located two streets to the right of the motel.

After that, hand in hand they walked to the place. Grace was still feeling the afterglow of married happiness in this small town with the man she adored. She was hoping any health issue of George was something able to be cured by following a diet, or adding more vegetables to their plan of eating.

***

A blossoming verdant park across the street filled the air with its perfumed aromas. George said, "It feels good to be out of doors. It was like being in a cage while I drove for hours on end. Is it all right if we don't get right back on the road?"

"Sweetheart, that's a great idea. I was feeling cooped up too. How about taking a stroll in the park after we eat?"

George smiled and said, "I like that idea."

Outside the bakery, several people were seated on striped chairs under the red and white striped umbrella-tables. They entered the bakery to select their food. The smell of freshly baked croissants filled the air. The aroma reminded Grace of how she thought Paris would smell, and she chose to have one of them with a cup of hot chocolate.

George ordered bacon and eggs, and coffee. After he paid the cashier, he was handed a small numbered ceramic pot. Then, he was asked to take a seat outside while they waited for their food to be prepared.

"This is a great way to start our day" he said, and grace agreed.

***

After their delicious brunch, they walked to the park. George read a signpost saying there were boats available to rent. "I'll rent a boat and row us around the lake."

They strolled down a path lined with tall old golden oak trees whose branches met overhead providing them with a shaded canopy from the bright sun.

Grace said, "This must be a lovely walk in the fall. On a clear crisp day, I can imagine sunshine streaming through a canopy of golden leaves as they start to fall across this path."

"I can see the boathouse at the end of the path" George said, and he ran ahead to rent them a boat. George chuckled as he removed his jacket, "In Chicago they'd call this "lake" a "big puddle.

Let's go see what's on the other side. Then, he handed his jacket to his companion, and she folded it. After that, he rolled up his shirt-sleeves. George helped her to be seated, and he started to row across the lake.

As he approached the middle of the lake George realized he was very tired. He stopped rowing. "Whew. this is hard work." Then, he pulled in his oars to rest. They sat drifting in the boat looking up at the fluffy looking clouds continually changing shape.

Often, they described to one another the figures they saw in the clouds. The noon sun beat down on them, and Grace splashed the cool lake water on herself.

After a while several small clouds came together, and George said it looked to him like an old-fashioned sailing ship he'd once built in a bottle.

"It's good to stop and rest when I'm tired. No one is looking over my shoulder telling me to hurry up. I feel free."

***

After he rested, he was able to row back to the boathouse. Grace said, "Sweetheart, I'm feeling sleepy after being out under the sun. I want to take a nap. Is it okay with you if we go back to the motel?"

Her heart leapt with joy when George replied, "Sure. I like being in bed with you."

At twilight, George awoke and went to the bathroom. He admired his new tan reflected in the medicine cabinet mirror. Returning to the bedroom he switched on the light. Then he was upset to see his companion's face, chest, and arms were now a bright red.

"You're red all over" he gasped.

"I wasn't wearing any sunscreen lotion out on the lake. My skin is sunburned. It hurts when I touch it. We need to go and get something to put on my skin right away." Grace pulled a loose-fitting dress over her head. "We must go to a drug store now."

In lobby she asked for directions to the nearest drug store from the desk clerk. After that they hurried to the car. En route to the druggist they passed the blinking sign "Cellarbration."

"I want to go there for dinner."

"Oh yes, I liked it in there too," she said

Grace was content in the knowledge her husband did still love her, and he found her physically attractive. She'd been worried when he stopped pinching her behind, and unhappy he no longer found her a desirable companion since he moved out of their bedroom.

The pharmacist recommended a spray tanning lotion. After Grace purchased it, they went back to "Cellarbration". Grace was able to navigate George to the restaurant.

Chapter 6

After entering "Cellarbration", Grace hurried to the restroom to apply the spray that would lessen her pain. Meanwhile, George stopped at the bar to thank the bartender for his help in getting them a room. They chatted amiably for several minutes.

Jack, the bartender, introduced himself. He asked George if he knew how to play chess.

George replied, "If my friend wouldn't mind, I'd like to play with you after we eat."

Then, the mustached maître di showed George to a table.

***

After a few minutes passed, Jack walked over to give George his copy of the local newspaper to read while he waited for his girlfriend. George scanned the paper until Grace came to the table.

"That burn spray works really well. I feel much better now. Sorry it took me so long."

"I'm glad you feel better. Jack, the bartender, gave me his newspaper to read while I was waiting for you. He has a miniature chess set with a rug board at the bar. If it's all right with you, I'd like to play a game of chess with him after we eat."

Grace was pleased that George was being considerate, and she said "It's all right with me, dear. I'll read your newspaper and try do the crossword puzzle while you're playing."

***

Grace selected and ordered the chicken quesede for their dinner. While they were eating, Grace noticed the blonde woman return to the restaurant. and she looked unhappy. She chose to sit at a table near the phone.

That pretty girl reminds me of my daughter Grace thought. It looks to me like she could use some distraction from whatever has upset her. When George leaves to play chess, I'll go to her table and introduce myself to her.

After dinner George left the table to play chess with the bartender. Then Grace rose and walked over to the pretty woman's table.

"Hello. My name is Grace Goodrich. My husband has gone to play chess with Jack. Do you mind if I join you?"

"Please do. I'm glad for your company. Let me buy you a drink Grace. Is a diet cola all right?"

Grace smiled and nodded as she took a seat. The young woman waved her arm and called out, "Estelle, bring two diet- cokes over here." Then she studied Grace's red face and said with concern, "I hope your sunburn doesn't feel as painful as it looks?"

"It did hurt a lot, but I used a spray the druggist recommended. Now, I feel much better. We didn't realize the lake in the park was so large. My husband tried to row across it, but he got tired right in the middle. So, we just sat out there watching the clouds changing shape until he got his second wind. That's when the sun got at me."

"Well, I'm glad the spray helped you, Grace. My name is Cindy Citron. I'm a photography model. In my line of business, I must be careful to stay out of the sun, unless I use a heavy-duty protective cream.

"I'll be sure to get some before I try to enjoy the sunshine here next time."

"People I meet think I'm very lucky, and my job is easy. However, they're wrong. It's a very demanding lonely business. I must diet all the time, exercise five times a day, and jog in the park every morning. Today, after the shoot, my photographer told me he'll need to retouch all my photographs to get rid of the age lines the camera sees. I'm only twenty-three years old. sigh.

"Cindy, I don't like to see lines pop out on my face either, but I've earned those stripes."

"Grace, I like your attitude. Would you like to come running with me tomorrow?"

"I'd love to jog along with you. after all the driving we've done I'm feeling the need to exercise my body. I don't know our check-out time at the motel. It's near the park."

"That's a terribly expensive place. I stayed there for ten days. Then, one of the photographers I work for told me the address of the building complex where I'm now renting a furnished studio by the month, and it's the same price I paid to rent that motel for the ten days I was there."

"Wow. that's quite a savings."

"How long are you planning to stay in town?"

"I'm not really sure. My husband retired a couple of months ago, and we're on our way to Albuquerque to see the "Hot-air balloon Festival". Grace sipped her drink, and then said, "We're both looking forward to seeing it."

"Oh Grace, it's just beautiful. It's so interesting to see how many people are needed to tend and fill up those balloons, but it's a very noisy place! It's thrilling when you see them launch a balloon in the air." Cindy paused to take a sip from her drink, "It's even more exciting if one of the balloons falter... and must come back down to earth for a repair. But Grace, the festival doesn't start until the middle of next month."

"Really? Is that so... please excuse me Cindy, but I need to go to the bathroom."

As soon as Grace went into that private place, she hurriedly looked in her purse for the festival ticket envelope. She slid it open with her finger to read the date.

Grace was shocked to see the date on the tickets was for next month... She'd assumed the tickets were for this Saturday, but they were for a Saturday next month.

Oh, I should've opened the envelope and checked the date when George handed me the letter when it arrived. Now, I feel foolish to have assumed it was for this Saturday. Driving back to Chicago is out of the question.

Grace thought, George will laugh at me for assuming incorrectly... but he needn't know I made a foolish mistake. George said he's tired of driving the car.

I'll just suggest to him we stay in this town until next month. In that way I can avoid his ridicule because I made a foolish mistake.

Cynthia was right to point out to me I assume that I know instead of attending to get the information and know the facts. I must stop assuming that I know the answers when I don't.

I'll slow down and ask for all the facts instead of jumping to conclusions without enough information. I must learn to confront and ask before I jump to a conclusion without evidence.

***

Grace returned to the table and said, "Cindy, I'm interested in renting one of those inexpensive apartments in your building complex. I'd like for us to stay in town until the festival opens next month."

"Let me see your newspaper, Grace."

She handed it to her, and Cindy turned to the real estate section and studied the page. "I don't see an apartment listed here, but I know one is available. It's only a short walk from here, but I'm waiting for an important phone call. So, I'll draw you a map and write the directions," and she did.

"Thanks for your help, Cindy, and the drink."

"I'm on the jogging trail at nine o' clock every day. Come meet me in the park for as long as you stay in town."

"I'll do that. So long, and it was very nice meeting you Cindy."

Chapter 7

G race walked over to the cherry mahogany painted bar to stand next to her husband. She watched the game in progress. The bartender's king was in check, and George used his knight to checkmate his opponent.

"Wow. That was an impressive game. You sure are a good player, George," said Jack.

"Excuse me gentlemen... George, I have something important to discuss with you. please come with me now."

"Okay. See you next time Jack."

"You make friends so easily. I wish I had your knack.

"I do what I like doing, and another person joins me, and becomes a friend. Jack is a partner in this restaurant.

"Whatever made them call this place "Cellarbration"?

"It was the cheapest location the owner's brother was able to afford. After he died in a car accident, the sister converted his bar into this restaurant. It's really a series of attached cellars under the stores above it.

Jack says everyone in town celebrates the big'n small events in their lives here. Jack started to work here after the death of his wife a year ago. Now, he feels like he has an extended family because he works here. Everyone in town comes in here to celebrate the big'n small stuff in their lives. Jack started working here after the death of his wife."

"Well, it was a clever idea to use a Mexican Fiesta theme to liven up an otherwise dreary cellar. George, I'm really glad to see you're enjoying our stay in this town. I read in the newspaper the balloon festival doesn't start 'til the middle of next month.

A customer here told me about an inexpensive furnished apartment complex. She rents one of them by the month. If it's okay with you, let's rent one of them until the festival starts. It will cost us far less to rent the apartment than to continue to live at the motel."

"Let's take a look."

"My friend drew me a map to show us how to get there."

"Let's go take a look". They got into the car and Grace navigated using the map Cindy drew for her.

In less than ten minutes they reached a red brick colonial complex with a swimming pool. "This place looks okay", they agreed.

After that, they went inside to the manager's office to find out if an apartment was available.

***

George stood looking out the kitchen window of their new apartment drinking his morning coffee. "I'm glad I found this town. The people here are smart and very friendly.

Last night, Jack helped me to understand that a person gets older, and never younger. All life changes need a period of adjustment and... and one change inevitably leads to another... and another.

I haven't replaced my activities with new ones yet. A job gave me something I liked to do. It was taken away from me. My job is gone. No one can go back to an earlier time.

Jack's wife died. I feel lucky that you're here with me. Jack can never be with his wife again."

"I'm glad he helped you to understand mourning the past makes it difficult to enjoy the present. Sweetheart, would you like a second cup of coffee?"

He shook his head and said, "I like doing things for the fun of it."

"George, you're a smart man. I'm sure you'll find community service rewarding. Well, I've finished drying the breakfast dishes. Shall we go for our walk in the park now?"

"It's a very friendly park."

"What makes you say that, George?"

"You asked me why some benches were painted gray, and others green, but I didn't know the answer. Last night Jack told me that when a person feels lonely in the park, and wants someone to talk to, then he or she sits on a green bench. But if you don't want any company then you sit on a gray one, and no one will talk to you."

"That's a very simple and friendly idea. I like this town too."

Chapter 8

The following month Grace reluctantly packed their suitcases. She'd been content all this time relaxing with her husband. Going to Paris didn't seem as important to her since they'd come to this small town. George had rekindled the romance in their dull lives It had surprised and delighted her. George was still eager to see the opening of the "Albuquerque hot-air balloon festival.

He put the bags she'd packed into the trunk of the car. After that, they got into the car and belted up. George removed the key from his tan trousers and inserted it in the ignition. The engine turned over, but then it gasped, and went dead.

George popped the hood and got out. He looked at the engine but he couldn't figure out what was wrong with the motor.

Watching him it occurred to Grace that in the future instead of hinting at what she wanted she would just tell him…not wait for him to figure out what she was hinting at.

She'd perspired through two blouses a day on their road trip. She didn't realize George hadn't noticed she was not comfortable while he drove. It wasn't fair of her to expect him to read her mind. I should've asked George to lower the temperature.

She realized it was important for her to make her needs known to others and take on the responsibility to ask.

***

Grace got out of the car and told George she was getting them help. She walked down the street to the grocery store and called Triple A for road service. Then, she purchased two iced cokes, and returned to the car.

George was still staring at the silent motor when she handed him a drink. Grace said, "it's a lucky thing for us our car broke down here, and not when we were out somewhere on the road to Albuquerque."

They waited more than twenty-five minutes until someone arrived to help them.

The triple driver got out of his tow truck and looked under the hood of the car. Then, he asked George to start the engine. He continued to examine the silent motor. After that, he looked under the car.

Grace overheard him tell George something had burned out, and he would need to send for that car part.

George told her it would take a few days before the part would arrive. Then, he removed their luggage from the trunk, and the driver towed away their car.

He carried the suitcases back to the apartment. Disappointed, George slumped onto the couch.

Grace said, "George, we're not going to miss the festival you want to see."

"The car is broken."

"A bus can take us to Albuquerque too. We'll just have to come back here for the rest of our clothes and the car before returning to Chicago.

Grace repacked, and then she consulted the bus schedule in the phone book. After that, they walked to the bus station. He carried the bags, and Grace purchased their tickets.

Chapter 9

The air-conditioned bus trip felt delightful to Grace, but George grumbled that he felt cold. After his complaint, Grace rummaged in the bag and got out his sweater.

***

As Grace stepped off the bus in Albuquerque a blast of dry heat greeted her. She staggered as if she'd been struck. Then, George helped her to walk to a bench inside the station.

Walking to the motel was simply out of the question. They took a cab to the motel where the travel agent had booked them.

It was close to the festival. The cab fare was nearly half the cost of one of their bus tickets. They checked into the motel, and Grace hurried to their room to shower, and apply her suntan lotion before going out of doors under the strong New Mexico sun.

Grace carried the tickets in her purse. She was glad that it wasn't necessary for them to wait on the long line under the blazing sun at the festival entrance to purchase tickets.

Once inside the gates they were impressed to see the festival area was at least the size of three football fields in each direction.

Nevertheless, the place was crowded with many colorful balloons being tended to on the ground, and others filled, and waiting to be launched.

Despite its huge size, it was a very noisy place. It surprised them to see crews of five to seven people were needed to inflate one balloon. They had no idea it took so many people to get a hot air balloon ready to leave the ground and rise into the sky.

They saw many striped, red, yellow, blue and green bulb-shaped balloons, and five more balloons in the shape of farm animals. several well-known companies had their advertising logos on many of the balloons.

Grace noticed "for sale" signs posted on two balloons. all the balloons were being readied to go up in the air.

It was exciting to see the balloons rise. Even more exciting to see one falter, and then return to the ground to be re-adjusted, afterward, it was re-launched. they found all aspects of balloon launching and handling interesting to see and watch in action.

However, Grace was surprised, and somewhat distressed when she realized that there was no control tower to signal who should wait, and who had clearance to go up, or come back down to the ground.

Grace thought this unsupervised sporting event was dangerous for the balloonists in the crowded air space above, and possibly for the spectators below.

George asked her if she would like to take a ride up in one of the balloons? However, after seeing one of the balloons nearly collide with another of the balloons filling the sky above, she replied, "No thank you."

***

Later in the day, they were dismayed to discover the line to get into the restroom was more than a twenty-minute wait. That was far too long a wait for a senior citizen, and Grace wet her panties while waiting on the long line.

Grace hadn't brought along a thermos, and so George purchased many glasses of sweet lemonade being sold by vendors throughout the day. Then, to their dismay they discovered there were no restaurants on the grounds. George had to pay a cart owner ten dollars for an extra-long hot dog for each of them. After he bit into it, he complained, "It's bad enough this hot dog cost so much money, but it doesn't even taste good even though I loaded it with onions, mustard, relish, and ketchup."

They looked forward to sundown in the hope that the air would become cooler in the evening. However, after a brilliant orange, pink and gold sunset it did get dark, but the air didn't cool down. Then, they agreed it was time to wearily drag themselves back to the air-conditioned motel.

***

The food served to them in the motel restaurant looked okay.

However, Grace found it to be too highly seasoned for her taste. She hoped George would complain and send it back to the kitchen.

She was surprised to see George eat the spicy food without any comment. So, grace picked at the food on her plate. Then she regretted that she didn't have the courage to complain and send it back herself.

Grace left the table to refresh her makeup after only managing to eat a few bites of the awful food she'd been served. Looking at her reflection in the bathroom mirror she scolded herself for eating any of that meal, and not sending it back to the kitchen. She'd been surprised that George had eaten the food without comment. Had the food tasted all right to him? Has he lost his sense of taste?

The waiter presented the bill to George. He reached into his jacket pocket, but discovered his wallet wasn't in it.

The waiter was irate to learn George had no credit card, or cash to pay for the meal, or tip him.

George was outraged to find he'd been robbed. He didn't know if it had happened at the festival, or in the crowded motel lobby. The motel-manager was summoned to the table.

When Grace returned, she learned what had happened. She'd started to carry along her own card since George started to have difficulty remembering where he put his wallet.

The heat and loud voices had given Grace a dreadful headache. She decided to rely on her husband to do whatever needed to be done, and left the table to return to their room to lie down and rest.

When George returned to the room, he told her the dinner bill had been added to the motel bill. Luckily, the travel agent had prepaid their stay, and George's card was on file.

Grace called the credit card company and explained what had happened. She was told the card company would accept only the motel charges and would then cancel the card. After that, a new card would be sent to their address in Chicago.

**

They tried to relax as they watched the television news. The weatherman on the program said, "Tomorrow will be clear and sunny with a strong wind. The temperature will be in the high nineties.

Grace said, "Maybe that's good weather for balloon enthusiasts to hear, but not me. The festival was very interesting to see, but it was too noisy, and too crowded to suit me."

"The lines were too long for everything" he said.

"Whenever I saw something that I liked I thought the price was far too expensive to buy it and be able to enjoy it."

They discussed whether they wanted to stay another day, or leave tomorrow. It had been an interesting trip to see the festival, but they agreed they were ready to go back to their apartment, and more comfortable weather. So, the following day they checked out.

Fortunately, Grace had brought along a blank check with her. She used it when she bought their bus tickets."

***

They were relieved to find the weather more to their liking when they returned. George said, "This is a nice place for us to live. I'm tired of driving the car. Can't we stay here?"

"Sweetheart, one place is pretty much like another place to me. as long as we have each other anywhere feels like home to me."

Chapter 10

Dear Diary,

I haven't made friends my age yet in this small town. It's pleasant here, but I'm lonely for my dear friends in Chicago. There're questions and problems a woman my age has that I want to discuss with girlfriends my own age.

Why do men look more distinguished as they age while women just look older? Does George find me less attractive now?

Is there something I might try to do to heat things up again?

A few weeks ago, I was thrilled when romance returned to our dull routine marriage. However, I got sunburned... after that, I thought George was being considerate not to try to romance me. However, I'm tan, and he hasn't even pinched, kissed, or approached me in bed. Why not? What was it that ignited that spark between us a few weeks ago?

***

Dear Diary:

I've racked my brain trying to recall each hour prior to our romantic encounter step by step. I wonder if I should play Sinatra records, or encourage George to drink whiskey sours at bedtime?

Chapter 11

In a few days they settled into a comfortable routine: Grace was again volunteering at the hospital gift shop, and George had volunteered to coach the high school track team. Each night they ate dinner at "Cellarbration".

Grace encouraged George to drink, but he wouldn't order any liquor. He told her he needed a clear head for his chess game.

***

Grace taught Cindy to knit after dinner they would sit together knitting caps for newborns at the hospital while George played chess with Jack, or one of the other patrons.

The wurlitzer jukebox provided them with pleasant music in a convivial setting throughout the evening.

***

One night grace said, "Cindy, you're a beautiful young woman. I'm truly surprised you have the time to sit here and knit with me."

"Grace, it's not easy for me to meet a man who will put up with my limited time schedule for dating."

"Barry, my son has the same problem. He complained to me as soon as he dates a woman more than three times, she becomes too demanding of his time. So, he's not bothering to date any more.

Dear Diary,

What's wrong with these young people of today? Marriage is a very important part of life. If they don't make time to date, then how will they find the right one to marry?

Could that be the reason why they marry and divorce, and then remarry and divorce so much nowadays?

***

Dear Diary,

I don't understand how young people can live happily without having a meaningful relationship in their lives along with having sex. I believe that's what being a human being is all about. A job is good to have, but it's not all there is in life.

I'm glad I never had their work ethic. It wasn't easy for me to give up my teaching career. However, I wanted to travel and go with my husband to all the places his company sent him. Grace re-read her diary entries to gain insight into what might be the cause of their lack of sexual activity.

After that, she started to believe it was more her problem than his. Maybe I should buy a vibrator and stop trying to persuade George to put down his book and come to bed.

***

Dear Diary,

My tan has faded. George is content living here. I still haven't figured out what turned him on at the motel. Perhaps I should suggest we stay there one night?

***

Dear Diary,

Barry has voiced his concern since we've decided not to return home. He is coming out here to see us as soon as his "active participation is no longer needed in a current case he's handling for his firm."

***

Dear Diary,

George was delighted to learn Barry is coming. He brags about his successful lawyer son to anyone who will listen to him at the restaurant while I sit and knit caps for the new- born with Cindy.

***

Dear Diary,

Jack asked me if I happened to know Barry's favorite dish and assured me it would be on the menu when he came. Then, I told Jack that Barry was my son too. Also, that I've been married to George over forty years.

Jack was very surprised. Why hadn't George told Jack I'm his wife?

***

Dear Diary,

I crocheted a copy of the fashionable tie worn by the CEO in the photograph taken with my husband at his retirement party for Barry. It looks great in the box I placed it in. I hope he likes it. I will pick up Barry at the train station tomorrow.

***

Grace's hand was shaking with excitement as she applied her make up. She was going to meet Barry's train this morning. She studied her yellow linen reflection in the door mirror to see if she could find a flaw in the way she looked. After she was satisfied, she drove to the train station.

***

Luckily, a car was pulling out just as Grace arrived at the station. It had been three years since the last time she saw Barry. She waited on the platform wondering if her son would think she'd changed very much.

Grace had arrived at the conclusion her age was the reason George was no longer interested in her. She ran a comb through her hair and was glad she'd chosen to keep the same shade of blonde she'd always used.

Her heart was beating fast with excitement, and she could hardly catch her breath as the train pulled in with a screeching halt, and a cloud of steam.

Grace saw several passengers leave the train, but her son wasn't amongst them, and she felt disappointed. Then, a frail looking man stepped down onto the platform.

It took grace a few moments to realize that the man was Barry.

"Son, have you been dieting? You're so thin I barely recognized you." She was concerned to see the dark circles under his eyes, and she wondered if he'd been ill.

He said, "Mom... you look as good as you always did. Where's dad? What's he doing?"

"Your father is coaching the high school track team. You'll see him later at the apartment. I made you a gift. it's in the car. I was lucky to get a space close to the station.

Grace thought... if my son didn't notice any difference in the way I look then why does my husband ignore me in bed? Is Barry just being kind to his old mother?

They continued to walk side by side to the car. When they reached the buick, she popped open the trunk, and he put his suitcase into the trunk.

"Mom, I'm sorry. I should've brought you something, but I went right from the office to the station."

"Just having you here is gift enough for me son."

***

Seated in the car, Grace gave him his gift. He unwrapped it and said, "Mom this is a wonderful tie. It's the very latest style. Thank you so much. " And he leaned over to kiss her cheek.

After that, he removed his tie, and put on the tie she'd made him. Grace was proud and glad he liked it. She thought it looked very nice on him.

***

After Grace parked the car, she led her son to the apartment. He took off his hat and put it on the clothing rack. Grace was shocked to see his hairline had drastically receded... George still had a full head of gray hair. However, she did not comment about it to Barry. She wondered if his diet, or an illness of some kind had caused his hair loss.

"I'm glad you like your tie son. Barry, I find it difficult to sleep on a train. Do you feel tired? Your father won't be home for hours. you have plenty of time to take a nap before he comes home.

"Mom, that's a great idea. where's the bed for me?"

She led him to the prepared pull-out-couch-bed, and then left him to rest. After that, she prepared a salad for her lunch, and then read a book.

Chapter 12

B arry was snoring when George arrived home late in the afternoon. She told him she thought Barry looked exhausted. She suggested that they let him sleep through the night.

However, George insisted on waking him. He wanted to show his son off at "Cellarbration".

***

While Barry showered and shaved, Grace voiced her concern. "Barry must be pushing himself too hard at his job."

"Being a success requires keeping your nose to the grindstone," said George.

At the restaurant Jack greeted Barry warmly, and invited them all to have a "welcome drink" at the bar. It amused Grace to watch Barry... wide-eyed staring at the restaurant's whimsically attired employees.

Then, she noticed Barry's eyes light up when he spotted Cindy. She was wearing a red turtle- neck sweater dress. Seated alone at the table near the phone.

Grace asked, "Barry, would you like to meet my young girlfriend in the red dress over there?"

Barry nodded enthusiastically, and they walked from the bar toward her table.

Grace started to introduce Barry to Cindy when he suddenly became red in the face, and gasped as if in pain. Cindy screamed and tried to catch Barry as he fell unconscious on top of her.

She attempted to keep hold of him, but he slipped out of her arms onto the red tiled floor.

A patron seated at the next table rose quickly and placed his seat cushion under Barry's head. After that, Grace bent to loosen his tie, and undid his top shirt button.

Jack hurried over to them. He saw Barry lay on the floor unconscious. Immediately, he phoned 911 and asked for an ambulance to come at once.

After that, Jack put his arms around Cindy and tried to comfort the crying frightened young woman. "Cindy, let me take you home."

"Grace needs me here."

"Cindy, my husband is here to wait with me for the ambulance. Let Jack take you home."

"All right, Grace. I hope Barry will be okay. After my run tomorrow I'll go see him at the hospital" and then she left with Jack.

Chapter 13

J ack was glad for this opportunity to be alone with Cindy, but she was so upset that he allowed this opportunity to ask her out on a date to pass. He said, "Good night" and left her.

***

Grace checked Barry's wallet to see if he had a medical insurance card with him. Then, she decided it was best to hold onto his wallet, and carefully removed his Rolex watch for safe keeping.

***

Ten minutes passed before the ambulance arrived. The medics entered the restaurant. Grace told them what had happened while one of the medics felt for Barry's pulse, and the other placed an oxygen mask over his face. After that they asked Grace to come along with them.

Grace told George to follow the ambulance to the hospital. The men carried Barry out to the ambulance and drove to the hospital emergency room. George followed them in his buick.

Barry was wheeled into the hospital as soon as they arrived, and Grace handed Barry's health insurance card to the nurse. Then she signed the admittance papers.

After that, Grace joined George in the waiting room. Then, they sat and waited for a doctor to come to examine their son.

George paced up and down the pale green linoleum lobby. He paused several times to ask the intake nurse when the doctor was going to come to examine his son.

***

After several interruptions, the nurse told George the doctor was with Barry. After that she suggested he go up to the private waiting room on the second floor. She assured George she would tell the doctor where to find him after he'd completed the examination.

Grace sat and stared out the waiting room windows watching the stars fade as the sun rose while George paced the floor. After several minutes passed, he stopped pacing to stand before Grace and sobbed, "If Barry dies it's my fault. I should've listened to you and let him sleep. you told me he didn't look well."

"Don't blame yourself. This would've happened to Barry while he was asleep. Then, we wouldn't have known to get him medical attention. It's because you coaxed him to come out with us that Barry is getting the help he needs. You saved Barry's life. "

***

The elevator doors opened. A man in a white jacket walked toward George and Grace. She took hold of George's hand.

The man cleared his throat before saying, "I'm doctor Lovitch. I examined your son. I did a cardiac catheterization, and the results were negative. His blood pressure is still elevated, and I want to do an EKG tomorrow to see how his body is responding to the medication he was given tonight.

The good news is his arteries are clear, and he didn't have a heart attack. It was, I suspect, an anxiety attack. I'll release him in a day or two."

"Thank you, doctor. Why did he have the anxiety attack?"

"I can't pinpoint the cause, but the dark circles under his eyes and his lack of muscle tone indicate to me this man works under a great deal of stress, and he sits too long at a desk. He hasn't been getting enough sleep, or exercise."

"Should he stop working?"

"Well… no… but I agree his work habits need a vast improvement."

"Barry dedicates himself to doing a top-notch job like you did George. He's got your work ethic."

"He's not a married man with a family to support. I don't want to bury my son because he was too devoted to a big city law firm."

"Too much stress is a relevant factor in most of these cases," said the doctor.

Grace cleared her throat and said, "George, if Barry thought you needed his help, he might move out here. It would be far less stressful for him to work in a small town like this one. Why don't you encourage him to set up a law practice here in town?"

George slapped his thigh and chuckled, "Grace you're a fox! I'll ask Barry to help me take care of you."

"George, you're older than me. Isn't it more plausible to say you're the one in need of his help?"

"Excuse me for interrupting you folks, but there's no need for you to argue. It's a fine idea. If you like, I'll advise him less stressful work is indicated for him, and a change of location would be prudent."

"Isn't that the truth?"

"Yes. After that, I'll suggest he consider living nearer to his aging parents."

Chapter 14

C indy had promised Grace to visit Barry after her run. True to her word she entered the hospital after her morning run. She walked to the information desk. "I've come to see Barry Goodrich. He was admitted last night."

The volunteer worker looked up the name of the patient in the information file. Then, she told Cindy the room number. Barry Goodrich is in on the third floor.

Cindy didn't attempt to use the elevator next to the desk. Instead, she asked to be directed to the nearest staircase.

Cindy feared being alone in a small, closed space. It was for this reason that she preferred to sit and wait by the phone at "Cellarbration" rather than stay alone in her one room studio apartment.

She walked past the gift shop in the lobby. The salesclerk was spraying the flowers in the window. Involuntarily Cindy shuddered. She recalled what the photographer had said to her last month... "From now on Cindy, I'll have to retouch the crow's feet and fine lines from your face when I photograph you in future shoots."

Cindy was already using every makeup trick she knew to camouflage those fine lines for her close ups. It upset her to realize the camera saw what time was doing to her face; despite her efforts to hide the aging tell-tale lines.

Opening the staircase entrance door, she began to climb the steps. Upon reaching the second-floor landing, a handsome young man wearing a white jacket with a stethoscope hanging round his neck joined her. He smiled at her and started to climb alongside the pretty blonde woman dressed in a powder blue jogging outfit.

"Hello. my name is Jerry Lovitch. This is how I manage to squeeze my exercise into my working day."

Politely, Cindy returned his smile and agreed, "Walking is a good exercise."

"Are you visiting a relative?"

"No. A friend."

"I'm glad to hear you say that. I'm a busy doctor, but a lonely guy. Please have lunch with me after you visit your friend?"

She chuckled, "You're also a very fast worker."

Please meet me in the cafeteria downstairs in an hour? What's your name?"

"Cindy Citron." She didn't like the idea of being an "easy pick up". However, she figured it was probably hard for a busy doctor to meet healthy women.

"See you in an hour Cindy," and he left her on the third-floor landing and continued to climb the stairs.

***

On the third floor, Cindy searched the hall for the correct room number. She found it hard to meet eligible straight guys in her line of work… she didn't want to wind up an old maid.

Today, I came to see one eligible young man, and met another…. a doctor no less. It's like granny says, "It doesn't rain but it pours." Life is full of surprises. Then, Cindy paused at the correct door- number and knocked.

"Come in" she heard, and opened the door. Entering the room she asked, "Remember me?"

"I was just thinking about you while I've been lying here. I hoped I hadn't scared you off."

Cindy smiled prettily and said, "Well… no one else has ever fallen at my feet after being introduced to me." And then they both laughed.

"I'm glad you came to see me, Cindy. Please sit down. Would you like some water, juice, or coffee?"

"No thanks. I'll just sit here and visit with you, if you're feeling up to it?"

"Looking at you Cindy, I can't help but feel better. Mom didn't need to tell me you're a model. A woman as beautiful as you must be a very busy person. I appreciate you taking the time from your busy schedule to come and see me."

She smiled, and thought her days were not as busy as they once were...or will be in the near future. They chatted amiably for more than half an hour before she left.

Afterward, Cindy walked downstairs to the cafeteria to meet Jerry.

***

From the cafeteria doorway Cindy easily spotted Jerry. He was seated at a table with three attractive young nurses. She was surprised to see he had plenty of opportunity to meet healthy women. She realized she was wrong to assume he didn't have the chance to meet attractive healthy women. I'm the one with limited opportunities. Time marches on, and my tell-tale age-lines will soon lessen future job opportunities for me to work.

It's time for me to think about a second career, or getting married and raising a family. My beauty routine can no longer be of first importance in my life.

Barry has made it quite clear he's taken with me, and I like him a lot. Grace told me her son is a successful lawyer with little time to date. Hmm.

Granny would advise me, "A bird in the hand is worth two in the bush." So, I'm not going to bother to have lunch with Jerry, and she turned and left.

Chapter 15

George and Barry were seated at the kitchen table while Grace prepared breakfast. The sun shone through the window making shadows on the wall of the potted plants she'd bought and placed along the windowsill. It gave the apartment a homey feeling.

Grace overheard her husband ask, "Son, what do you think about the boy who was taken downtown by the police at the scene of this crime? I know he's a good kid, but his family has no money to hire a lawyer. Please son, would you talk to his parents? Give them some free legal advice."

"Dad, let me see the newspaper. Barry read the news article and said "This boy was only brought in for questioning. He hasn't been charged with anything. How come you know him?"

"He's one of the boys on my track team. It makes me feel good to be important to them, and it's fun for me to be there."

Grace said, "Cindy helps me knitting caps for the new-born at the hospital."

"Isn't Cindy a great gal? My job is all I have the time to do now. I miss the way; it makes me feel to be of service to others and have fun while doing it. Don't you think Cindy is a gorgeous woman?" "Well, she's a good looker son, but is she smart enough for you?"

"We went to the movies last night. She has a keen sense of humor."

Grace said, "Well, she must be smart if she went out with you."

"We're going on a picnic today."

George said, "if you need a few dollars to take her out properly, I'll be glad to give it to you son."

"Oh George, a picnic sounds like fun. Don't you remember when we used to go to the lakeshore for our picnics?"

"The newspaper says rain later in the morning."

"Oh, that's all right. We'll figure out something else to do if it rains."

The foggy morning soon became a light rain. Barry took an umbrella from the stand at the door when he left. He walked to the liquor store on the next street to buy a bottle of merlot. After that, he went to Cindy's apartment, and pressed the doorbell.

She greeted him at the door barefoot and dressed in a pink and yellow flowered dress. Cindy smiled at him. Then, Barry felt his heart warming at the sight of her. She took the wine he'd brought, and he trembled when her hand brushed against his hand.

Quickly, he carried the wet umbrella into the bathroom. He opened it and placed it in the tub to dry. It amused him to hear a Doris Day recording of "It's a lovely day today" playing on her phonograph when he returned to the living room.

He saw Cindy had spread out a green quilted blanket on the living room floor, and there was a picnic hamper beside it.

He chuckled, "I see you don't intend to be deterred by the weather. However, don't you think we'd be more comfortable if we sat at the table?"

"No problem" she said, and swiftly bent over to lift up the wicker hamper. Barry was seized by a desire to grab Cindy and kiss her passionately. However, he was able to constrain himself with great self-control.

He thought the timing was not yet right. He uncorked the merlot at the kitchen counter to let it breathe and said, "Spending the day with you Cindy makes it a lovely day for me."

She smiled and said, "Barry you say the nicest things. are you hungry yet?" He wanted to grab her and cover her with his kisses, but he said, "I'd like to dance with you before we eat."

He thought it a natural way to get her into his arms. He didn't want her to think he was an oversexed animal who would take advantage of being here alone, and scare her off.

"Looking through her records she asked Barry if he wanted a rumba or a tango?"

"A tango is perfect." Ah, the dance of love. I hope dancing close will get her in the mood for romance. Cindy selected a phonograph record and put it on.

The rain began to beat harder against the windowpanes. Barry felt his heart racing as he waited for her to come into his outstretched arms. I'm glib with words, but my mind goes blank when I'm near her. Perhaps as we dance closely, she'll understand I'm yearning for her. I want her to want me as much as I want her.

After Cindy put on the tango record, she walked into his waiting arms. He firmly placed his hand at her small waist and pulled her close to his body. Cindy could feel the heat rising from his body, and it aroused her.

Barry moved her body skillfully to the sensuous strains of the music, and his firm control of her body was thrilling to her.

The raging storm outside orchestrated the pounding of their hearts as they moved in unison to the strains of the music. Cindy had never before felt this excited with a dance partner.

She was sorry when the record ended but pleased when Barry kissed her neck and face. A streak of lightning flashed across the blackened sky startling her. At the sound of a loud bang of thunder Cindy threw her arms around Barry's neck drawing him close.

Barry didn't want to let go of Cindy. She excited him as no other woman had before, but he wanted to be careful not to rush her. Alone in her apartment he didn't want her to think he'd force him-self against her will. He wanted to go slow and be sure of how she was responding to him.

He said, "Let's eat, I'm horny... I mean hungry." Cindy was pleased to hear his slip of the tongue but pretended she hadn't heard it.

The roast chicken she served at lunch was tender and delicious. They devoured it noisily. Afterwards, Barry helped her to wash and dry the dishes.

Then, they sat with their wine glass in hand on the couch. Cindy showed Barry her family photograph album lying before them on the coffee table.

Barry enjoyed sitting beside her warm body and thought it was wonderful to see the photos showing her change from a scrawny little kid to the beautiful woman next to him.

***

After seeing her grow up from one page to the next, Barry felt as if he'd known Cindy longer than a mere week. He said, "I noticed the name "zipper" on many of the pages in your album. was that your brother's nickname?"

After he said that, Barry saw a pale red blush was creeping up Cindy's neck to her cheeks. She replied softly, "No. it was my nickname. When I was a little girl. my brother used it to tease me with it all the time."

"Why did he think to call you that?"

"One day he saw my shadow on the pavement, and he joked, Cindy's shadow looks like a straight line. I bet if she stuck out her tongue she'd look like a zipper." Everyone laughed and agreed.

"That's how it became the family joke... until I was seventeen and won a beauty contest, and a modeling contract."

"Oh, you poor kid. It must've hurt your feelings to be called "zipper" all those years growing up."

"At the time it did upset me, but I've forgiven them all now."

"Well, I haven't forgiven my little sister for calling me an "egghead". She was born blonde, beautiful, and athletic. I was the klutzy dark-haired brainy older brother.

Linda won the prize cups my father bragged about to his friends. Dad lavished her with his attention, and showed off her cups in the office, and kept some in the living room on the mantle.

"I was the brainy one, but it was Linda who delighted my father by winning trophies at sporting events. while I just stood around watching him shower her with praise and affection."

"I'll bet you excelled on your report cards."

"Sure. I made the honor roll all through high school, and earned a scholarship to go to college, but dad never showered me with any affection on account of it."

"Barry, I'll bet you that Linda was envious of your good grades."

"What? You think Linda has been jealous of me? That thought never entered my mind." Hmm. Can that be the reason why I feel happy and proud of myself whenever Linda comes to me asking me for my help? I give her money whenever she needs it. Am I really helping my sister when i give her money, or am I keeping her dependent on me? Could it really be that I'm showing off my ability to her? Does she believe that I'm truly the stronger one between the two of us?

There's more to life than being a money-making-machine. Money can't really buy love or affection. I'm starting to understand I've been cheating myself all these years… and possibly delaying Linda from becoming responsible for herself.

Doctor Lovich told me it's time to live closer to my parents. It's also time for me to stop trying to help my sister. I need to live my own purposeful life.

I can begin here in this town. I'll live nearer to my parents. I'll no longer stay at a job where I must work overtime in order to be able to be of financial support to Linda.

Barry ended his long silence and said, "Cindy, I'm considering opening a law office in town."

"Oh Barry, I know your folks would love it if you do it."

"Would you like it?"

"Oh yes. Then we could see one another more often. I'd love it."

"I want to see a lot more of you too," and Barry leaned forward and tenderly embraced her. She placed her arms around his neck and drew him closer. He covered her with his warm moist kisses and pulled her tighter to his hot body.

Cindy returned his kisses with enthusiasm, and then yielded to his blossoming passion as they slowly sank onto the soft green quilt beneath their bare feet.

Chapter 16

A heavy rain was falling. There were few customers. Jack was wiping the glasses behind the bar. Then, a young man entered. Jack saw he had a black band on the sleeve of his suit

It reminded Jack of a similar night a year ago when he came in out of the rain with a band around his arm after burying his wife, and the unborn baby. He motioned to the young man and poured him a drink at the bar, "On the house" he said.

The surprised young man took the drink and swallowed it in one gulp. Then, he started to cough, and Jack poured him a beer chaser.

"Thank you, he said. "I needed that."

Jack said, "Sit at a table if you want to eat or drink more." and the young man did. He picked up the menu on the table.

Jack was concerned by not seeing Cindy seated near the phone for a few days. He wondered why she wasn't sitting in her usual place. He thought if I ran the world, things would stay just as they were. The first time Cindy walked in the door, I liked her, but thought it too soon after the death of my wife to ask her out for a date. He didn't feel ready to be good company for a woman until now.

Jack decided the very next time she came in he would ask her for a date. He'd really liked the way things were in here and wondered what had happened in the universe to change things.

He didn't want anything here to ever change. Everything was perfect the way things had been. What's happened to change the dynamics of the old routine?

Estelle walked to his table and took his order.

Jack had wondered why she hadn't married one of the fathers of her three children. Then, one Valentine's eve her current boyfriend wept at the bar. He confided to him,

"Estelle keeps turning down my marriage proposals. I love the woman" and want to marry her. Then, he begged Jack to put in a good word for him with Estelle.

However, Jack overheard Estelle brag to a girlfriend "With three fathers paying child support I've been able to buy a house, a car, and start to save up money for my children's college education." And Jack understood to mind his own business.

The restaurant door opened, and Grace and George entered. Jack asked, "How's your son doing?"

"Barry's all right now, Jack. It seems my boy works under too much pressure at his current job. I'm going to try to convince him to stay here and open a law office in town."

"We could use another lawyer. The one we have here now is planning to run for mayor in the next election."

George said, "Thanks for telling me that Jack. It might be an important piece of information in his decision. Are you ready to play a game of chess?"

"Sure. Let me wipe off the bar before I spread the rug for our game.

**

Grace walked over to the jukebox and selected several tunes. Then, she took a seat at a nearby table to listen to the music and she started to knit. Her thoughts turned to Barry… her loyal loving dependable son.

Grace was relieved there were no longer dark circles under his eyes, and he'd gained a few pounds. Each morning now Grace was enjoying waking up and making breakfast for her men.

She hadn't realized how much she missed the role of "mother hen." It gave her a cozy familiar feeling to prepare food for her loved ones. Grace was glad George was happy coaching the track team.

A shadow fell across the table and Grace looked up. She was surprised to see Jack had come over to her table. She smiled wryly and asked, "Has George beaten you more quickly than usual?"

"That's not why I came over here to talk to your Grace. George is not acting like his usual self."

"What do you mean Jack?"

"George insists on moving his bishop like a knight. At first, I thought he was joking with me. However, I realize now he isn't joking. Grace, I don't mean to upset you, but I think something is not right with your husband. I'm no longer going to play chess with him."

"What you've described is certainly strange behavior for George."

"Grace, the wife of a friend took him to see a doctor when he began to act differently. Perhaps you should take George to a doctor."

Grace thought, perhaps George is not pretending when he doesn't seem to understand my sexual innuendos... oops.... darn, I dropped a stitch... then, Grace's cell phone started to ring, and she answered it. "hello".

"Mama, you've got to talk sense into Barry right away."

Grace immediately recognized her estranged daughter's voice. A warmth of relief and gladness swept through her. "Linda, I'm glad you've called me. But I don't understand what're you talking about. How can you know what Barry needs when he's living here with us? Where are you?"

"After Barry told me you'd left for New Mexico, we've been living here at the house in Chicago."

Grace was shocked to hear Linda reveal this information. It made her realize Barry knew all along about Linda's whereabouts.

Nevertheless, he'd allowed her to worry needlessly all this time. Hump! is that the behavior of a loyal loving son? "Why is it that you're calling me Linda dear?"

"I love my brother, Mama. I don't want to see him make a foolish mistake by marrying a girl he's known only a few days."

Grace was shocked to hear this unexpected news. After a long pause to gather her wits she said, "Linda, I'm glad you're safe. I was very worried about you. You're wise to have called me. I'll try to do my best, but as I recall... me trying to talk sense into you didn't do much good."

"Mama you were right on... I was too ashamed to admit to you I'm pregnant, and I had to marry Dallas. Please try to help Barry. Do you have any idea who this girl might be?"

"As a matter of fact, I think I do. Linda, I'm overjoyed to know you're safe. I'll do the best I can with your brother. Thank you for calling me sweetheart. We were really worried about you. We love you, Linda. I'm glad to know that you're safe.

***

Took a few deep breaths after the surprising phone call from her daughter. She thought George will "hit the ceiling" when I tell him Barry has withheld the information about Linda's whereabouts and allowed us to be unnecessarily worried all this time.

She would share this good yet shocking news with George, but dreaded being the cause of seeing George upset and hear him yelling.

She'd forgotten what Jack had said as soon as she heard Linda's voice. Grace decided tomorrow she would select a private yet public place where she would calmly tell George about Linda's phone call, and Barry's betrayal.

Chapter 17

After breakfast, Grace decided to use one of the gray benches in the park as the ideal place to divulge her information to George. She suggested to George they go for a walk in the park, and he readily agreed.

The birds were chirping, and a gentle breeze caressed them as they strolled hand-in-hand on the path beneath the oak trees. Then, Grace suggested sitting on one of the gray benches.

After they were seated, Grace turned to her husband and said quietly, "Linda is safe. Barry knew it. We were worried about her all this time, but he didn't tell us where she was. He knew Linda had left home because she's pregnant."

After that, Grace braced herself apprehensively fearing his tirade.

However, what she heard wasn't the reaction she anticipated from George. This man seated beside her after hearing this awful news said, "That's interesting."

Grace was stunned by his innocuous response. She carefully studied the dear face of the man she'd known and loved for over forty years. She was baffled by his casual response. Then, she recalled what Jack had told her about George not moving his chess piece correctly.

Now Grace realized this man beside her was unlike the George she knew. George would have understood the information she had just given to him. It was obvious to her this man was not acting like the man she'd married.

Tears came to her eyes as she realized Jack had been right to tell her George was not acting like the George they knew. Something indeed very wrong with this man sitting beside her behaving like a polite stranger after hearing about an important family matter. Grace wondered how far down into an unknown abyss had this George slipped? Could he be coaxed back? She knew she must do something right now... but what?

Grace took his hand, and in a gentle tone of voice asked him, "Do you feel all right George?"

"I'm fit as a fiddle. I don't want to be too far from a doctor."

After he said that, Grace agreed with him. Then, she said, "I'm taking you to see your doctor right now."

Chapter 18

The intake nurse at the hospital emergency room remembered George. She heard Grace complain that her husband was not responding normally to what was happening around him. She wanted for him to be seen by a doctor, and evaluated to determine the cause of his new behavior.

The nurse checked the roster and saw Dr. Lovitch was on duty this afternoon. He had an opening on his schedule. So, she directed Mr. and Mrs. Goodrich to the doctor's office on the second floor of the hospital.

Then, she phoned the doctor to tell him of the wife's concerns about a new patient on their way up to his office.

***

Doctor Lovitch was waiting at his office door. He recognized this couple. "Please be seated ma'am and wait here while I examine George. I'm leaving the door open so you can hear us.

After that, he asked, "Is anything worrying you George? Come in to my office and tell me about what's troubling you."

"Doc, this wedding band tells me I'm a married man... but where's my wife? I'm worried about her."

"Who is the lady sitting outside waiting for you George?"

"I think she's the cook where I live. "

Grace was shocked to overhear what George had told the doctor, and could hardly believe her ears... George had stopped treating her as a wife weeks ago, but she didn't know why until now. What was wrong with his memory?

She realized now she had to be the one to confront Barry. She was furious with his betrayal of her trust.

The doctor called her into his office after George's examination. "Mrs. Goodrich, I was able to determine your husband has senior dementia. I suspect it has advanced to Alzheimer's disease since he doesn't know that you are his wife, but I haven't tested him for it.

It's vital for you to understand this is not the beginning of your husband's disease. I'm sorry to tell you the progression of his senior dementia started some time ago. I strongly advise you to try to place your husband in a gated facility for his own safety as soon as possible. It may take some time.

"Does he get lost frequently yet?"

"Well, I've noticed it takes George longer and longer to come home."

"For his safety, I urge you to place George in a gated facility as quickly as possible."

"Our home is in Chicago. we're only renting a place in town."

"Great. There're many excellent places there Mrs. Goodrich. In this town there's always a long waiting list for the two facilities we have here."

"Doctor, my friend had to place her mother-in-law in a facility for Alzheimer's disease three years ago. She carefully researched several places."

"That's fortunate. Although this disease affects one in five families there're many people unfamiliar with Alzheimer's disease. I suggest you contact her right away. I'm glad you understand the necessity of placing your husband in a locked facility as quickly as possible for his safety.

I'm going to give you a prescription for aricept. It's a drug that helps delay the onset of Alzheimer's disease. Unfortunately, no cure yet exists for this disease. George will never regain the memories Alzheimer has already stolen. They've simply been erased from his mind.

It's like the ocean tide that comes in and carries away the sandcastles young children build on the beaches. The tide comes in, and carries them away.".

"I'm sorry I didn't bring George in sooner to see a doctor, and get him aricept. It would've given us more time to enjoy his retirement together. Thank you for your advice, doctor. I'll call my friend right away for the information I need. Then, I'll make arrangements to return home."

"That's wise of you, Mrs. Goodrich. You'll prevent George from getting lost and upset, or harmed."

***

After lunch, George took his nap. Grace used this opportunity to call Cynthia. She told her friend what had happened since they left Chicago, and then about this morning's visit to the doctor.

Cynthia said, "I'm very sorry to hear George has senior dementia." Then she said if he no longer remembers you're his wife it's probably Alzheimer's disease.

"Yes," Grace agreed. "That's just what the doctor said. Cynthia, I recall a few years ago you and John needed a place for his mother at a facility. Is she still there? How do you like the place you found for her?"

"John's mother was content there. Recently however, Sylvia lost the memory of how to swallow. They've been feeding her through a tube. She doesn't like that at all. She begged me to have them stop her tube feeding... I can no longer bring myself to go there to see Sylvia now.

I never thought to say this Grace, but I'm glad John passed away two years ago, and he doesn't have to witness what's happening to his mother.

You'll need the names of the facilities I selected and liked. I'll go and get the file from my desk. Do you have a pen and paper ready?"

"Thank you, Cynthia. You're a woman of great courage. I'm sorry you have to go through this ordeal alone."

"Grace, I miss you. I'm glad you're coming home. Be sure to leave your name wherever you call. Be prepared to be put on a wait list. One in five families are affected by this disease."

Chapter 19

George awoke, and Grace drove him to the track field. There she arranged with one of the boys to bring him home George after practice. After that, she returned to her apartment and started to phone the places Cynthia had given her.

***

It was very discouraging to learn each of them had long waiting lists; however, she entered George's name at each of them.

Grace was very discouraged, and she prayed for guidance. She decided to make one more call to place her husband before she gave up for today.

She phoned the Seven Oaks nursing home…."Hello. my name is Grace Goodrich. My husband's doctor told me I must place George in a secure facility for his own good right away."

"That sounds urgent to me. We just had a cancellation, but I can hold that space open for your husband until tomorrow's posting."

"Oh yes! I want that bed space for him. We'll take the overnight express train to get to Chicago. George will be there in time. Thank you!"

***

As soon as she hung up then Grace phoned the train station to purchase passage for two to Chicago on the express train. However, to her dismay she learned only one space was still available. But she booked it for her husband and arranged passage for herself on the next train to Chicago. After that, Grace called her daughter.

"Linda, she sobbed, "Your father has Alzheimer's disease. He needs you to meet him in Chicago tomorrow morning at Union Station. I was only able to get one space on the express train. You must meet him at the Union train station. Then, take him to the Seven Oaks nursing home. Cynthia has the address. They've accepted him as a patient on the condition he be there in the morning...a sob caught in her throat... Linda, it's imperative you meet him at Union Station in Chicago. I arrive on the next train. Your dad no longer remembers I'm his wife. Linda, she sobbed, I'm relying on you to meet your father. This is urgent.

"Mom, I'm proud you're trusting me to do something this important for you and dad. I'm willing to meet daddy, but I have no money for a cab."

"Ask Cynthia for a loan. If he should give you any trouble tell him his wife is waiting for him at the Seven Oaks Nursing home.

"Mom, have you spoken to Barry yet?"

"Your father's illness is a sudden crisis. I've been busy all day trying to get him proper medical attention. I'm angry with Barry for not telling me your whereabouts, but I will take care of the matter before I get on the train tonight."

Chapter 20

Cynthia counted out a large portion of money from the "Emergency money jar" she'd dumped onto the kitchen table when Linda asked her for the money.

"Cynthia, I hope this is not an imposition on you."

"What're friends for if not to help one another? I have an appointment Linda, or I'd go with you, or at least lend you, my car."

"Mom said dad has forgotten who she is. Is she kidding me?"

"No. She's not kidding you. Alzheimer's disease steals away the memories from the mind of the victim. He may, or not remember you, Linda. It would be wise if you ask Dallas to go along with you."

"Okay, I will. Thanks for the money. It all sounds kind of creepy. I'll go and ask Dallas to come with me now."

Chapter 21

Grace pushed Cindy's doorbell and waited, but no one came to the door. She was about to leave when she saw Cindy's car enter the driveway, and park. Cindy got out of the car very slowly. Grace suspected that she was crying.

I guess Cindy has troubles she must confront too. Grace waved a "Hello" Then, she waited at the door for Cindy to join her.

While she was waiting, Grace thought sadly George's retirement was supposed to be the pinnacle of our well lived lives. He'd proudly told me he'd set aside enough money for us to live comfortably for the rest of our lives, and travel too.

I was so excited when he told me he'd arranged for us to go to Paris. Then, I was very disappointed to learn he wanted to go to see the hot-air balloons instead.

Now, I'd be thrilled if he could remember that I'm his wife. We worked hard all our lives for this retirement. My husband isn't really here now anymore; only his polite facsimile of the person I married. It just isn't fair what's happened to our lives!

***

"Cindy, I'm leaving town this evening, and I promised my daughter to talk with you before I left about Barry and you."

"Grace, you look very upset. Please come inside. I'll make tea for us."

Grace burst into tears and took a seat at the table. She sobbed

"Cindy my husband doesn't know I'm his wife! He has Alzheimer's disease. He thinks I'm the cook where he lives.

The doctor told me his disease has been going on for a long time. But I didn't recognize what was happening. Now, I need to place him in a facility right away for his safety."

"Oh Grace, how awful for you. I'm so sorry to hear your terrible news" and she hugged her. Then, Cindy gently patted her on the back to comfort her. After that, she put the tea kettle on the stove. When the tea kettle whistled, Cindy prepared their tea.

Grace saw Cindy wiping away her silent tears. "Why're you crying Cindy?" she asked.

"I... I just got unexpected news from a medical test i took last week. I haven't figured out what to do about it yet."

"You don't look ill to me, Cindy."

"I'm not sick, Grace. Don't you worry about me. Let's concentrate on finding a facility for George."

"I did find a place for him Cindy in Chicago, but it's on the condition that I can get him there in the morning. There was only one express train ticket available. I bought it for George. My daughter is going to meet him at Union Station in Chicago. She'll take him to the Seven Oaks nursing home. I'll follow on the next train.

Cindy, I've come here to say goodbye, and to ask you a question.

Grace took a sip of tea then asked, "Isn't it too soon for you and Barry to consider getting married?"

"What!? Grace, Barry has never proposed to me. I was surprised that I fell in love with your son so quickly... but I don't think my father will allow me to marry him.

"Is it because Barry hasn't got a successful law practice yet?"

"No. That's not the reason. It never occurred to me when we met at the restaurant that you weren't Catholic."

"I assumed you to be Lutheran, Cindy."

"Grace, I never expected to fall in love with your son. Today, I learned that the rabbit died. I don't know what I'm going to do about it yet."

"You'll marry my son despite your father's prejudice."

"Grace, I do love Barry, but I also love my dad."

"Seeing his daughter happy should be of more concern to him now than how to worship the lord."

"I'm having lunch with daddy after church Sunday. I'm planning to tell him about Barry at that time."

"Being in a family way may sway him. Don't you think?"

"You don't know my dad as I do. It's been five years, and he still hasn't spoken to my brother for leaving the seminary."

"Oh dear, life is so complicated," said grace. I was only able to get one ticket on the express train to Chicago. Fortunately, Linda can meet George, and take him to the facility. I was lucky to get him in there without waiting on a long list. But it's on the condition he's there by noon. I'm leaving town tonight on the next train to Chicago."

"Grace, you'll need help to pack and arrange for the transporting of your car to Chicago."

"You're right Cindy. I forgot all about the car."

"Let me help you. I'll pack for you while you prepare dinner for George. Then, I'll drive you and George to the station. After you put him on the train, I'll wait with you for your train. Tomorrow, I'll arrange for your car's transport. Let's go to your place now. You can get together the papers required for the transit and give me the address it will be going to in Chicago."

"Yes. That's a good idea, Cindy. I'll need to phone a car transit company and find out what papers are required. Cindy, I want you to know it would please me very much to have you for my daughter-in-law."

"Grace, I'll pray for a good outcome for all of us. I'm planning to tell my father about Barry after Sunday services."

"Cindy, I suggest you see your dad before church on Sunday."

"I'll pray on that suggestion too."

Chapter 22

C indy packed everything for Grace and for George while Grace served dinner to George. Then, Cindy took the two suitcases to her car. After that, she waited for Grace and George to leave their apartment and come to her car.

***

Grace knew she needed George's cooperation to come along with her, and get on the train to Chicago. She said a prayer to calm herself, and a simple idea occurred to her... George was worried about his wife she'd overheard... so Grace made up a story she would tell George.

After dinner she said, "George, your wife called. She needs your help. You must go to her right way. You can take the express train to Chicago tonight".

"All right. I'm ready to go and help her."

"Cindy is waiting in the car to drive you to the train station. I'm going with you to the train station."

"Okay."

***

The train pulled in, and Grace searched for a porter. "My husband needs to ride on this train to Chicago. He has Alzheimer's disease. Don't worry, it's not catching. Please be sure he meets our daughter, Linda Goodrich with his luggage. This is a photo of her. She'll be waiting on the Union Street station platform." After explaining all that to him, she gave him ten dollars.

"Don't you worry ma'am; I'll look after him good." Then, he took the suitcase from her. After that they walked over to George, and she introduced them to one another.

The porter took his ticket and helped George to find his place on the train. George didn't wave to them from his window. Grace and Cindy waited on the platform until the train left the station.

Chapter 23

Grace's train wasn't due to arrive for two hours. She suggested to Cindy they have dinner at a small cafe near the station. Standing in line to be seated they overheard many upset townspeople talk about the recent rape of a young female runner in the park.

Neither Cindy nor Grace joined in this topic of conversation. Each of them had a lot on their own mind to think about.

Soon they were seated, and ordered dinner from the menu. They went through the motions of eating their dinner, but neither was hungry.

After dinner, Grace assured Cindy she'd be all right to wait alone for her train. She asked Cindy to take care of her plants. After that, they hugged and said "farewell."

***

Grace sat alone on a wooden bench in the empty station house. She was feeling sad and angry about the way things had turned out in her life. She muttered, "George's retirement wasn't supposed to be like this."

Grace felt cheated by what Alzheimer's disease had done to her husband; stolen his memories. She was uncertain about her future. The cost of George's health care was going to be expensive. She realized there was no one for her to depend upon now but herself, and the Lord. Grace hoped she had the survival skills and courage to live her life alone. Then, she removed tissues from her purse and wept.

***

Grace boarded the train when it arrived. A porter placed her suitcase up on the rack above her seat. After she'd settled in the soft embrace of her seat, she opened her purse and withdrew her diary.

Dear Diary,

I thought all there was in life was to be charitable, nice to people, and look as pretty as a picture so that I'd attract a successful handsome man who would want me for his wife. I thought I'd succeeded and found the loving kind of life I wanted with my husband. Now, I discover that I've been robbed of my life by Alzheimer's disease.

I liked my photo that George placed on his desk; and the photos with our babies on the piano in the living room. It was like an award for being who I'd become... a loving devoted wife, busy mother, a kind person, and a good friend and neighbor.

Now, a new road has opened before me that I never imagined I'd have to travel. I must re-examine myself to determine who I am without my husband. I don't really know what to do yet. Do I have the courage to survive this new journey at my age?

Mending a broken heart is more easily done by two, but I am alone. I pray for guidance to do what is needed a day at a time. Then, she put her diary back in her purse.

Thank you, Lord, for the good life I've enjoyed all these years. Thank you for my good health. Please guide me now. Amen.

***

Grace was startled to be awakened by a conductor calling out "Chicago. Last stop." She'd been rocked to sleep by the soothing motion of the moving train. She got herself ready, and managed to pull down her suitcase. After that, she departed from the train.

On the platform she was relieved to see a long line of taxis. She joined the line of passengers, and engaged a cab. Grace told the driver the address of the Seven Oaks Nursing home.

Then, she wondered if he was going to refuse to take her there because a strange expression came over his face when she told him the address.

He said, "Yes, maam. Will you be checking in?"

"No. I just want to make sure my husband got there earlier today. My daughter met him earlier and took him there."

"In that case, I'd better wait for you. It's difficult to get a cab at this time in the morning."

"Not if you're going to let the meter run while I'm in there.'

"If you pay me when we get there, I'll stop the meter. Then, I'll have a smoke and stretch my legs while I wait for you."

"Thank you. It's really considerate of you to suggest you wait for me".

***

The driver pulled up to the Seven Oaks home. It was a very large, impressive place. The fifteen-room main house stood on a large manicured grassy hill, and the property was fenced in by a tall wall with a grilled iron gate. Grace thought the owners must've bought this property from a wealthy estate sale.

She paid the driver and got out of the cab to ring the bell in the wall, and state her business. After that, the gates swung open. She got back in the cab, and he drove her up to the front door.

The door opened as Grace left the cab. A sleepy looking woman about fifty was standing there to greet her. "Hello, Mrs. Goodrich. I'm Alice Adams... the director here. I've been waiting for you to arrive."

"My daughter brought my husband to you in time?"

"Yes, she did. She explained you had to take a later train.

However, she would not sign the admission papers for George. At the moment he's in a wheelchair waiting to be admitted. Your daughter said she was unable to assume the responsibility of paying for his care. You'll have to sign him in now."

"Yes. Please, let's get the paperwork done now."

"My office is to the right. follow me, please."

***

Grace didn't bother to read the myriads of papers, but quickly signed them because she was grateful her husband was accepted here. "What time is visiting hours here?"

"Mrs. Goodrich, you won't be able to see your husband for thirty days."

"Why not?"

"We've found new patients require that amount of time to adjust to the schedules here, and make new friends... if and when possible."

"Well, Alice, I thank you for waiting up for me. I'll be back in thirty days."

Grace gave the driver her home address, and then relaxed. She was pleased she'd been able to get George into this nice-looking place. The cost was far more than she'd expected to pay for his care, but George had earned the money. He deserved good care.

Linda left the porch light on for her mother. Grace paid the driver and doubled his tip. To her surprise he returned some of the money saying it was too much. Then, he handed her his card and said, "Call me when you need a cab."

"Thanks for your help... Grace read his card... Dan." He carried her suitcase to the door, and then waited 'til she unlocked it and went inside before he tipped his cap and left.

Grace was weary. She left her suitcase in the foyer and went upstairs to the master bedroom. She flipped on the light switch, and saw her bed was occupied by Linda and Dallas... this was the only king-sized bed in the house.

She turned off the light and went to Linda's room. Grace lay across the bed fully clothed and was asleep before her head touched the pillow.

Chapter 24

Grace awoke to the chirping of birds, and the aroma of fresh brewing coffee. She saw her suitcase had been placed inside the room. She stretched herself, and then went to the bathroom.

A cup of coffee seemed more important to Grace than showering and putting on her makeup. She went downstairs to the kitchen. Through the open door she saw Dallas was flipping pancakes.

"Hey, I'd like one of those please" she called out to him.

Deftly Dallas put one on a plate, and placed it on the open table setting as she entered the kitchen. Then, Grace saw Linda was seated at the table... she had a blackened eye.

Grace demanded to know, "Dallas, did you give that shiner to my daughter?"

Linda replied, "No Mama. It was daddy who hit me when I went over to greet him at the train station."

"Didn't you tell him you were there to take him to see his wife at Seven Oaks?"

"Mama, I was just so glad to see him that I ran over to kiss him "Hello" ..."

"That's when he punched her. I pushed her out of the way before her dad could hit her again. After that, I grabbed his arm, and he started to yell he was being kidnapped..."

"Dallas had to punch daddy again to quiet him down. That's what made Don come over to us. He asked, "What's going on here? I'm an off-duty police officer.""

"I told Don what you'd told me to say mama... about his wife waiting at Seven Oaks, but dad kept yelling he was being kidnapped. Mama it was just awful."

"Don was really nice to us. He offered to drive us to Seven Oaks," said Dallas.

"I drove, and we made daddy sit between Don and Dallas in the backseat. Don gave me the instructions to drive there.

When I stopped for a traffic light daddy tried to jump out of the car."

"Mrs. Goodrich, for a man his age he put up a real tough struggle. When we got there, we needed the help of the orderlies to get him into the building. They had to strap him into a wheelchair to wheel him in."

"Mom, Alice asked me to sign him in, but I had to refuse the responsibility of paying them for his care. I told her you were on the next train... You'd been unable to buy two places on the overnight express train."

"What a terrible time for all of you."

"After all that, Don was kind enough to drive us home. I gave most of the money I borrowed back to Cynthia. It's a good thing that I listened to her and asked Dallas to come with me. It was awful. I still can't believe daddy doesn't know me. I never heard of Alzheimer's disease."

"George doesn't remember me, and I'm his wife." After saying that Grace wept for a few minutes.

Linda asked her mother if her father's room was nice, and Grace replied, "I haven't seen his room yet."

"Mom, will you be going there to see daddy today?"

"No. New patients aren't allowed to see visitors for thirty days. They need that time to learn the new routines and make friends there."

Dallas said, "It will give us time to figure out what we're going to do next... right Linda?"

"Mom...I didn't like living with Dallas's sister on the ranch. We don't have any money. Can we stay here?"

"Yes, but you'll both need to get jobs. I can't afford to support you. you'll have to figure out how to support yourselves. I need to pay for your father's care, and I must support myself too."

"Didn't daddy save enough money for his retirement?"

"I hope he was able to save enough to cover the Seven Oaks bill, and provide for me. The company sends him a retirement check each month. I must go to the bank today. I'll find out what my money situation is then... I've always left the financial matters to your father. Meanwhile, you need to get a newspaper and start your job hunt today."

"Mom, Dallas doesn't have a car anymore."

"You'll both need to get jobs. I can't afford to support you. Mom doesn't stand for "made of money". You'll have to figure out how to support yourselves. I need to pay for your father's care, and must support myself also."

"Didn't daddy save money for his retirement?"

"I hope he saved enough. At the bank I'll find out what my money situation is. I've always left financial matters to your father. "Mama, we don't have any money. Can we live here with you?"

"What? Quickly, Grace realized it was because of a lack of money Linda had to return home. "Linda, I've always left the finances to your dad. I'm not sure if i can support myself after paying for George's care. You're both welcome to sleep here. However, you'll both need to get jobs as soon as possible. Then, she opened her purse and said, "Dallas, here's five dollars. go out and buy a couple of newspapers so you can both check out the help wanted ads today."

"Mom, Dallas doesn't have a car anymore."

"The buick won't be delivered here for a few days."

"I'll walk with him. Dallas doesn't know where they sell the newspapers."

Chapter 25

I t was with a heavy heart that Cindy inserted the key to her father's redbrick colonial home. She'd decided to see her dad before Sunday services as Grace had suggested.

Unexpected, she quietly opened the door. She saw her father was waving a newspaper in his hand while talking to several seated senior members of the church. He was denouncing the rape of an innocent girl who'd been jogging in the park.

"Our church does not condone abortion. Therefore, we must be ready to support this unfortunate girl so she can get medical attention. If a child should result from this dastardly deed, then in good conscience, we must try to find a home for the infant, and not shun her. We must not forget she's a victim, and so is her unborn child. There must be no shaming of her if she comes forward and needs financial help.

I will be the first donor to the fund I am proposing for this rape victim. After that, he wrote out and dropped his check into the basket on his desk. The others agreed with him, and more checks were added to the basket as it was circulated around the room. Then, the filled basket was left on his desk, and the group rose and left the library pleased to have contributed to a worthy cause.

***

Cindy held the front door open for the guests as they departed. She heard the murmurs of praise for her father to have championed this unfortunate young woman. She was proud of her dad too.

Cindy wondered how far his sympathy for a rape victim went. Might it even extend to her?

An idea occurred to her as the last guest departed. Cindy started to whimper and weep. Her father hurried to her side and asked, "What's wrong with you?"

"Daddy, I'm the girl in the park who was raped." She could see his face register a look of shock and pain on hearing her words.

He said, "Oh no" and pulled her into his arms and stroked her hair. "I'm so sorry this happened to my little girl. I'd like to kill the bastard who did it, and he hugged and rocked her for several minutes.

Cindy had never lied to her father before and her heart was racing.

***

After a few minutes he said, "The police need a description of the man who raped you."

"Daddy, he hit me over the head from behind. It happened while i was on the jogging trail where it curves down a slope with tall those thick bushes near the tunnel entrance… As I was about to enter the tunnel, I heard a noise behind me. As I turned, I felt a painful blow to the side of my head. I crumpled to the ground.

Then, as I was losing consciousness, I felt someone dragging me further into the tunnel. I wasn't able to cry out or do anything about it."

"How will I get us justice if you can't identify him?"

"Dad, I never saw him. I only remember falling on the ground. When I didn't arrive to have lunch with my friend… she and her brother searched for me. They found me in the park tunnel and carried me home. Daddy, I was glad to hear you say you understood the raped girl is a victim and should not be shunned."

"It's the only Christian path to follow. I hate to have this rapist get away with his crime. However, I see no reason for you to come forward if you can't help the police catch him…and further humiliate yourself."

"I'd like to forget it ever happened."

"I wish there was some way I could help you Cindy," and he lowered his head and wept.

"Daddy, I've been seeing a boy who says he loves me. He wants to marry me. However, I recently discovered he's not catholic. He's lutheran. Barry wants to come and see you to ask for permission to propose marriage to me."

"Oh?" he commented and stroked his chin. "It's only fair that you tell him what happened to you."

"Daddy, Barry loves me. I don't think it will matter to him why you give your consent... I'll do whatever you think is best for me."

Then, Cindy watched his face contort as he came to his decision. It took only a few minutes, but it seemed like an eternity to Cindy as she held her breath waiting for him to speak.

"Tell this young man all the facts. After that, if he still wants to marry you, bring him to me after services next Sunday."

"Yes daddy. You're a wise man. I'll do just as you say." Cindy's heart was beating wildly... does the end justify the means she wondered? She'd never lied to her father, and she wanted to go to confession as soon as possible.

Chapter 26

Barry and Cindy went to look at office furniture at the department store on Main Street. He was surprised to see the prices were far more costly than he'd anticipated. Barry didn't want to go into credit card debt this early in his career.

Cindy suggested, "Let's go see what's available at a used furniture store for your office." Then, she drove to the salvation army family store.

***

Barry searched the aisles to find what he thought should to be in his office. He was glad to find what he needed to be in good condition. However, all the wooden furniture he found were not the same kind of wood nor color.

Barry said, "I like the prices here. So, I'm willing to paint them all to match." After that, he paid for the furniture and lamps and arranged for delivery the following day to his new office above Main Street.

"Cindy, coming to this place was a great idea. Let's buy wine, and pizza and go back to my place to celebrate." Barry was sad that his parents had returned to Chicago and weren't there to celebrate with him tonight.

***

Cindy gathered her courage and sighed deeply as he poured her a second glass of wine. Then she said," It was a surprise to me we fell in love so quickly Barry."

"Life is mysterious and totally unpredictable" he said.

"In a few weeks it will become obvious that I'm pregnant. So, Barry, I'm asking you now to talk to my father this Sunday to ask his permission to propose marriage to me."

"We're having a baby Cindy?"

"That's what the rabbit test showed."

"Wow! I'm thrilled to know I'm about to become a father. Of course, I'll speak to your father this Sunday. I'll agree to anything he says. Darling, come here, I want you in my arms. I feel so proud and happy. Thank you, Cindy. Thank you!"

After he'd hugged and kissed her several times he said, "We'll need to start saving money for our baby. How soon can we get married my darling?"

"Well Barry, you'll need to ask for my father's consent to propose before I can set a date."

"The way you say it sounds like you think your dad may have an objection to our marriage. Is it because I haven't set up my law practice yet?"

"No. that's not it. Daddy is a devout Catholic, but your family is Lutheran."

"Wouldn't you marry me even if your father didn't approve?"

"I don't honestly know. I've never done anything without daddy's approval."

"Don't you love me enough to stand up to your father?"

"Barry... each time I see you I like you more and more. I feel so good whenever I'm with you."

"Doesn't that tell you to spend the rest of your life with me?"

"Oh yes! I would love to marry you, but I love my family too. If I go against my father's wishes I know he'd ostracize me like he did my brother when he left the seminary."

"Give up your studio apartment and come live with me after i speak with your father. I'll agree to anything he says."

"That's a good idea my darling."

***

Barry was no longer a partner in a law firm with many clients seeking aid. He carefully read all the articles in the newspaper hoping he'd be able to sell his services to someone who could use his expertise.

Chapter 27

Tomorrow Grace would be able to see her husband. She studied her reflection in the bathroom mirror. George always liked it best when I wore my hair in an upsweep. That's how I'll fix my hair for tomorrow's visit. Then, she went to her closet and pulled out his favorite black form-fitting silk dress. Hmm. I'll need to wear my high heels with this dress.

Grace wanted to look especially appealing to her husband. She was hoping he would fall in love with her again, or at least want to get to know her. It would be well worth the effort if he fell in love with her for a second time.

***

As she dressed Grace pondered on the fact that past unhappy life events came along with important life learning experiences. What had at first seemed a harsh life challenge to her had led to a better understanding of herself, and others. Life is a mysterious journey with unexpected discoveries and challenges. She was hoping this would continue to hold true.

***

Her son-in-law had a job with a cab company now, and Dallas offered to drive Grace to Seven Oaks. However, she'd already engaged Dan to take her there.

Linda still sported a bruised eye, and said she wasn't ready yet to see her dad again.

Dan beeped his horn to let Grace know he was waiting for her. He was very impressed seeing her beautifully dressed as she left the house to walk toward his cab. Hurriedly, he got out of the car to open the passenger door for her.

"You look very nice, Grace."

"Thank you, Dan. I'm ready to go to visit my husband."

Dan took a fleeting look at Grace in the rear-view mirror before he left the curb. He pitied her for what might happen to upset her when she saw her husband today.

***

Dan had placed his pretty red-haired wife, Doris, in Seven Oaks one year ago. After two months of begging him to take her home she became sullen and silent, and then sat staring out the of sunroom window.

***

Three days ago, Alice Adams called to tell Dori that she was no longer staring out the window. Hoping to talk with her, Dan rushed right over to see his wife. After he got to the nursing home he hurried to the sunroom. Dan saw a handsome new patient was seated and staring out the window now.

His wife was talking to another patient. He walked over and said "Hello" to Doris. She said "hi" and invited him to sit on the couch. He leaned over and kissed his wife's cheek a "friendly hello".

Doris gasped and pulled away from him. Then, she ran over to another patient. He patted her arm assumingly. After that, he walked over to Dan and asked him to leave Doris alone. Then, the man told Dan to leave, and he did.

***

Dan parked his cab at the seven oaks building, and then opened the door for grace. He warmly wished her "good luck".

Alice was at the front door to greet Grace. "Thank you for your patience, Mrs. Goodrich. I'm glad to tell you that George no longer thinks he was kidnapped. He's made friends here. You'll notice one in particular. Please try to understand Alzheimer patients have lost their memories, and much of their self-confidence. Occasionally, they're lucky and find new relationship to fill their loneliness for a little while until...

"Excuse me, Alice, but I haven't seen my husband for thirty days. May I see him now?"

The director became red faced, "Of course". she said and glanced at her wristwatch. "It's eleven thirty. The patients are in the sunroom. We'll walk down this hall and then to the right. I'll walk along with you."

Grace's high heels clattered against the tiled floor like ice cubes in a cold drink until they came to the glass doors of the sunroom. They paused and through the doors Grace easily spotted her husband. She was shocked to see her non-smoking husband lighting up two cigarettes.

George had always detested cigarettes. She started to smoke after he left their bedroom to punish him. Now, Grace's jaw dropped open in surprise.

She saw him hand one of the cigarettes to a red-haired patient. Then, she saw him kiss her cheek. Angrily, Grace asked the director, "Do you encourage that kind of behavior?"

Alice replied, "We neither encourage nor discourage it. Alzheimer's disease has robbed our patients of their memories."

Grace thrust open the glass doors and walked directly over to confront her husband. She stood angrily before him with her hands on her hips and demanded to know, "What's going on here?"

George looked up at her with his clear blue eyes, and then said calmly and unperturbed, "Hello. Would you like a cigarette?"

In that instant all that the director had been trying to tell her became crystal clear. Her husband had absolutely no idea who she was, nor that he was a married man. He had no understanding that he was doing anything wrong.

Confronted by this truth, Grace was both pained and shocked. then, she turned and hurried out of the room sobbing. She ran to the cab and told Dan to take her home.

"You look like you could use a drink, Grace. May I take you to a place I know before I take you home?"

Grace burst into tears and nodded her consent. Dan handed her a box of tissues. Grace got into the car, and he drove to a quiet cafe he knew overlooking the lake. The lunch crowd had left, and it was too early for the cocktail crowd.

Dan led grace to his favorite table next to the window with a beautiful view of Lake Erie. A waiter came to the table, and Dan ordered a seven and seven. Then the waiter asked Grace for her preference." I'll have the same" she said.

"Are you hungry?" he asked.

She shook her head and wiped her eyes. After that, she opened her purse and took out her compact. She opened the case to look in the mirror and started to laugh. Her mascara had run, and she was a streaky mess.

Grace snapped the case closed but didn't hurry to the lady's room to wash her face. She didn't really care how she looked at this moment.

"Was your husband staring out the window?"

"No."

"Was he sitting with a pretty red-haired woman?"

Grace stopped crying and sat bolt upright. She asked "How did you know?"

"Grace, I placed Doris, my pretty red-haired wife in seven oaks a year ago. She kept getting lost, and I had to go to work. At first, she wanted to go home. After that, she just stared out the window. She didn't know me. It was awful. Alice and I tried to help her make friends, but she would not, or could not.

Earlier this week, Alice phoned to tell me Doris was interacting with other patients. I went to see her right away. I was hoping she'd remember me, but she didn't.

When I kissed her on the cheek, it scared her. She ran over to another patient to complain to him. Then, that guy walked over to me and told me to leave. It made no sense to me to make a ruckus, and so i left. I guess that's when they became "good friends."

"Dan, in all the years we were married my husband never cheated on me, and he always detested cigarettes. I only started to smoke to punish him for moving out of our bedroom.

The director told me she neither encourages nor discourages patients to become "good friends". I don't like my husband staying there with her while I continue to pay his bill."

"Would you rather George sit and stare at nothing outside the window day after day? Grace, your husband no longer remembers that you're his wife. If he did, he wouldn't be cheating on you."

"I love my husband. It really pained me to see George kiss another woman."

"You're remembering your husband as he was before Alzheimer's disease stole his memories of you. Today, George doesn't know you at all.

Grace, you say that you love your husband. Are you going to take him away from where he has made a new friend? It may make you feel better, but aren't you being selfish to deprive George of a friend when he no longer has memories of you? He doesn't know you're his wife, or recall that he's a married man."

***

The waiter came with their drinks and placed them on the table. "Excuse me, Dan. I need to use the ladies room."

***

Grace returned to the table after she'd repaired her make-up. "It's hard for me to accept that my husband doesn't know me after forty years of marriage. But I do agree this George has no idea who I am. It would be vain and selfish to deprive him of his new friend because I'm jealous of a man who no longer knows me. Thank you, Dan."

"Grace, I must confess that I'd feel just as you do if I hadn't seen the bleak life Doris had staring out the window day after day. at nothing. It's hurting me too that they're friends, yet I'm happy for her."

***

After Dan drove her home, Grace went to see Cynthia. She told her what had happened at the nursing home, and of the chat she'd had with Dan.

"Grace, I recall when our husbands were working together, they each arranged for a long-term health insurance plan. It should be paying for George's care at the nursing home, and not you.

"Really? That would relieve me of a tremendous financial burden. I'll call his insurance man tomorrow. Thanks for telling me about this Cynthia."

***

Grace entered her house through the kitchen as the telephone started to ring. "Hello mom" said Barry when she answered it.

Grace asked, "Why did you never tell me Linda returned to the house after we left?"

"I was afraid you'd tell her to get out, and there was no other place for her to go."

"Didn't you realize that I was worried about my daughter?"

"No, I didn't. I thought you were too angry with her to be rationale about her situation."

"Well, you should've told me. Barry, you underestimate me. I love my children."

"I'm sorry mom."

"Don't assume again that you know what I'll do."

"You're right, mom. I'm truly sorry I underestimated you."

"I accept your apology, Barry."

"Mom, I opened my law office in town, and I'm seeing Cindy's father this Sunday to ask for his permission to propose marriage to her."

"That's wonderful news, Barry. I'm glad for you son."

"We want to get married as soon as possible."

"That's a good idea. I'm looking forward to your wedding. I'll tell Linda about you and Cindy... unless you want to tell her yourself?"

"It's okay for you to tell her, mom. Thanks for asking me about it first. Bye now."

***

"Cindy, I didn't realize it before, but my mother has matured a lot lately. She confronted me on my actions. She made me realize I had underestimated her."

"Well, she's been going through a lot right now. I admire her strength, courage, and determination."

Barry was taken aback by her assessment of his mother. "What do you know about my mother that I don't?"

"Didn't she tell you your dad has Alzheimer's disease? That's why she had to hurry back to Chicago. She persevered and managed to get your dad into the Seven Oks nursing home."

"What? When did she find out he had it?"

"Last week, after she took him to the doctor. Grace was only able to get one overnight express ticket to Chicago. Your sister met your dad at the train, and then took him to that facility. I assumed you must've known about it. Barry, you 've been living there with them all this time."

"Well, I didn't notice anything about my dad having a mental disease. I don't understand why my mother didn't tell me."

"Maybe you should ask her?"

"No. I'm going to call Linda and ask her why she didn't tell me what was happening. I thought we two were close."

Chapter 28

"Linda, how come you didn't call to tell me when dad got sick in the head?"

"How was I to know you didn't see he was acting weird? You were living right there with them for crying out loud. Didn't you see it for yourself?"

"What're you talking about? My father seemed okay to me."

"Did he know that you're his son?"

"Yes, he did. He even offered me money to take out my girlfriend. Then he asked me to talk to some kid's parents because he thought the boy was in trouble. What's wrong with our father?"

"Barry, he doesn't know mama is his wife. He thinks she's the cook where he's living. When I met him at the train station, he didn't know that I was his daughter. He socked me in the eye when I kissed him "Hello"."

"What?"

"Barry, he doesn't know mama is his wife anymore. He didn't remember me at all, and she started to sob. When he punched me at the train station, he thought I was trying to kidnap him. Dad has been at the seven oaks nursing home for a month now. Mama went there today to see him."

"Does he know her now?"

"Barry our father has Alzheimer's disease. It's not like he has amnesia. He's lost his memories of me and mom. He's forgotten me she sobbed. He's never going to know me again."

Slowly, Barry replaced the receiver on the telephone. A few moments passed while he tried to absorb all this information. Then, he dialed his mother.

As soon as she picked up the phone he asked, "Mom, why didn't you call and tell me my father has Alzheimer's disease?"

"At the time the doctor informed me I was furious with you for not telling me Linda's whereabouts when you knew that I was worried about her."

"er... I understand better now. And I am sorry about that. My sister said you went to see dad today. how is he?"

"George is now smoking cigarettes. He has a girlfriend at the facility, and he doesn't remember who I am. Other than that Barry, your father is in good health.

"Good grief! I can hardly believe you're talking about my father. He never smoked. He doesn't know you mom? I know he loves you. It sounds like he's in a mad world of his own."

"No, Barry. George is not crazy. He has Alzheimer's disease. It has stolen his memories of us from his mind. There's no cure for it. Remember when we used to build sandcastles on the beach?

We were able to enjoy them until the tide came in and washed them away. Well, Alzheimer' disease has entered George, and stolen your dad's memories of himself, and all of us too. Just like the ocean washing away the sandcastles we built."

"If I have my wedding in Chicago would dad be able to come?"

"Barry, George doesn't know me, or Linda. I don't know if he still remembers you, or not. I'm sorry to be abrupt with you son, but I've had a difficult day, and I want to rest now. There's a great deal for me to think about… and many bills to pay."

"Mom, would it help you if I went back to work for that law firm I left?"

"That pace of work was killing you, son. It's enough that I'm mourning my husband while he's still alive, and in love with another woman. I don't want to lose you too.

Stay where you are Barry. I haven't decided whether I'll be coming back to live near you, or remain here in Chicago and live near George "and then she wept.

"Don't cry mom. Remember you're not alone in this situation. We'll see this thing through together. You always told me to pray because it's always the darkest before the dawn."

He hung up and asked himself aloud, Am I so wrapped up in myself I don't pay attention to what's happening to the people around me that I don't see they repeat themselves, and fall asleep while reading? But aren't those things normal?

Barry prayed aloud, "Lord, please help me to find someone somewhere who can heal my father."

Grace had informed Cindy there was no cure yet for the Alzheimer's disease victim. Only a delaying tactic of the progression of the disease by using the drug aricept. Cindy saw Barry's body start to shake with sobs and went to him.

She decided not to tell him now that there was no cure for Alzheimer. She was mortified by her own self-centered thoughtlessness. She'd never mentioned to him about his father's disease, nor helping Grace to start his dad on the journey to the Seven Oaks Nursing home in Chicago.

Cindy realized she'd been involved with her own problem all this time and overlooked everyone and everything else. How selfish and self-centered I've been she thought.

Now, all she could do was to try to try to comfort Barry. She went to him with a heart full of love... and took a box of tissues with her.

The End

www.ingramcontent.com/pod-product-compliance
Lightning Source LLC
Chambersburg PA
CBHW082106140626
46553CB00018B/1095